D1615428

Building Sight

 **HMSO**

Published by HMSO and available from:

HMSO Publications Centre
(Mail, fax and telephone orders only)
PO Box 276, London SW8 5DT
Telephone orders 0171 873 9090
General enquiries 0171 873 0011
(queuing system in operation for both
numbers)
Fax orders 0171 873 8200

HMSO Bookshops
49 High Holborn, London WC1V 6HB
(counter service only)
0171 873 0011 Fax 0171 831 1326
68–69 Bull Street, Birmingham B4 6AD
0121 236 9696 Fax 0121 236 9699
33 Wine Street, Bristol BS1 2BQ
0117 9264306 Fax 0117 9294515
9–21 Princess Street, Manchester M60 8AS
0161 834 7201 Fax 0161 833 0634
16 Arthur Street, Belfast BT1 4GD
01232 238451 Fax 01232 235401
71 Lothian Road, Edinburgh EH3 9AZ
0131 228 4181 Fax 0131 229 2734
The HMSO Oriel Bookshop
The Friary, Cardif CF1 4AA
01222 395548 Fax 01222 384347

HMSO's Accredited Agents
(see Yellow Pages)

and through good booksellers

Peter Barker
Jon Barrick
Rod Wilson

Building Sight

A handbook of
building and interior design solutions
to include the needs of
visually impaired people

London : HMSO
in association with
Royal National Institute for the Blind

Published in the United Kingdom by
Royal National Institute for the Blind
224 Great Portland Street
London W1N 6AA and HMSO

Registered charity number 226227

© RNIB, 1995

ISBN 011 701 993 3

Design and production: June Fraser ARCA FCSD
Illustrations: Mark Booth BA (Hons)
Line drawings: Allen Cull FCSD
Photography: RNIB Library, Barry Dunnage, June Fraser
Copy editors: Jeremy Myerson, Graham Vickers

Processed by Graham Powell
The Facilities Group
81 Whitfield Street
London W1A 4XA

Printed and bound in the United Kingdom by
Offset Colour Print
159-179 Empress Road
Southampton SO2 0JW

Contents

Foreword

Sir Duncan Watson

This book, produced by RNIB, is intended to fill a gap in the range of literature available to the designers, developers and managers of buildings and interiors concerning the needs of disabled people.

It is based on practical knowledge of building, converting and operating a wide range of premises used by people with some form of visual impairment.

It also draws upon RNIB's 125 years experience of providing an advisory service to professionals and organisations working in areas such as housing, schools, hospitals, leisure facilities and public buildings. Throughout, many visually impaired people have contributed their valuable thoughts and experience.

The book sets out to explore the particular problems facing visually impaired people in the built environment. But, more important, it provides solutions too, and in a comprehensive reference section recommends the type of good design that sets out to include as many people as possible.

Far from restricting good designers and architects, the ideas in this book - particularly those concerning the way in which people with impaired vision perceive the world around them - indicate how the design

6

professions might create environments that are both aesthetically pleasing and more accessible to all users.

If those objectives are to be achieved, then everyone - architects, designers, planners, developers and building managers - should regard this publication as essential reading.

As we move forward from a post-war period of architecture that has sometimes failed us on the most basic levels, there is now renewed interest in creating buildings and public spaces that respond to our real needs.

We believe that designing for people with a disability is often a salutary reminder of what any good building design should always seek to achieve - namely, the creation of attractive, efficient and enjoyable places that enhance and enrich our lives.

Sir Duncan Watson
President, World Blind Union 1988-1992
Chairman, Access Committee for England 1989-1993

Introduction

**'Many barriers are put in the path of people with a visual
impairment - our task is to dismantle them.'***

RNIB exists to challenge blindness. We seek to do this in
two ways:

by providing services that help visually impaired people to
determine the quality of their own lives;

by questioning society's assumptions - and therefore its
attitudes, behaviour and actions - concerning people with
visual disability.

Visual disability operates on many levels. Personal
difficulties may be overcome - or at least minimised - with
the type of help that RNIB offers. However barriers arising
from uninformed attitudes and an unsympathetic built
environment often pose more intractable problems. These
can only be solved through a process of education and
information.

Over the past 20 years there has emerged a growing
awareness that good design - whether of buildings, interiors
or products - should by nature be inclusive. Of course it
would be impossible to design any environment to the exact
specifications of every minority group, each with its own
individual demands. However it is perfectly possible to
create environments that embrace and invite the widest
possible range of users.

*From RNIB's mission statement, 1993

8

Achieving this will often depend upon the underlying attitudes and decisions of planners and developers, and for this reason it is our hope that the messages in this handbook will also reach those decision-makers who have the power to encourage or impede the work of enlightened architects and designers.

Too often a token planning gesture towards disabled people seems to add cynicism to thoughtlessness: the ramp that provides wheelchair access to an un-negotiable building; the braille invitation into an environment that, once entered, proves positively hostile to visually impaired people.
This said, there is evidence that much can be achieved by sensitive and informed design.

Most housing organisations, architects and building project managers now recognise that inclusive design not only enhances the quality of life for everyone who uses a building, but that it also says something about the cultural values of the supervising organisation.

This handbook is intended to be of help to those responsible for shaping the environment in which we all live. Whilst recommending that the widest possible range of disabilities should always be taken into consideration, no apology is made for concentrating on the needs of people with visual impairment. Other publications have dealt with the needs of physically and sensory impaired people, but there are very few books dealing directly with visual impairment.

Meanwhile, the number of adults who are blind or partially sighted in this country has been conservatively estimated at nearly one million[1], an incidence of around one in 60 people. For those over 75, the incidence of visual

[1] Bruce, I., McKennell, A. and Walker, E. Blind and partially sighted adults in Britain: the RNIB survey Vol. 1, HMSO, London 1991.

impairment is around one in every seven people. For those between 65 and 74, the figure is around one in every 24 people. The number of older people will rise during the next 30 years, due to demographic changes now occurring in British society. The conclusion is inescapable: we must design for an older population, and therefore we must design for people with some visual impairment.

This publication reflects knowledge, expertise and experience gained by RNIB over a long history. It is presented in two distinct sections. The first - Design Principles - looks at the different types of visual impairment which affect people's relationship with the designed environment, and explores the broader ethical and philosophical directions underlying our recommendations. The second - Design Practicalities - takes a closer look at particular problems and gives step-by-step advice on design specifics relating to the way in which visually impaired people negotiate different exterior and interior spaces.

It does not claim to be a final work on the subject - experience tells us that as circumstances change so must our responses - but it is certainly the most comprehensive work on this subject to date. It provides answers to many of the questions that RNIB is regularly asked, whilst acknowledging that on some topics - particularly lighting - more research will have to be done before we can arrive at informed recommendations.

Most of the ideas in this handbook can be integrated into new building projects. Many can be economically incorporated into an existing building through routine maintenance or refurbishment. Opportunities must be

10

taken, wherever they occur, to meet the needs of visually impaired people.

Every thinking designer of buildings and interiors will agree that architecture holds up a mirror to society. Just as the modern architecture of the early years of this century reflected a new-found fascination with technology and the machine, so now there is an opportunity for contemporary building design to reflect the strong groundswell of social concern that exists for the interests of all members of society, including those physically, sensorily or mentally disadvantaged in some way.

In many cases, the sensory, physical or mental impairment of an individual is not the primary handicap. Rather it is the assault course represented by the built environment that poses the most serious threat to independence and full social integration. If the ideas in this book are taken on board by those responsible for the built environment, then many people with a visual impairment will be freed to enjoy a much fuller life. Until then the effects of thoughtless design continue to erode the interests and rights of visually impaired people in almost every area - housing, employment, education, recreation, leisure and transport.

Our philosophy is to advocate design for all - and that means design that reconciles the needs of visually impaired people with the general scheme of things. Only when this kind of thinking enters the mainstream of building design can we begin to claim the equality of opportunity which should surely be the hallmark of any civilised society.

Design Principles

This section introduces the underlying ethical and philosophical arguments which shape the design suggestions in this handbook.

Each chapter explores the spatial and environmental implications of the different types of visual loss which people suffer. Design principles are established on which practical recommendations can be based.

Chapter 1
Inclusive design

There is a certain type of design approach that sets out to include as many people as possible. It does not look for the lowest common denominator, nor does it attempt to reconcile the often conflicting needs of every possible minority group in society.

Rather, by considering many varieties of special needs inclusive design tries to break down unnecessary barriers and exclusions. In doing so it will often achieve surprising and superior design solutions that benefit everyone.

One of the objectives of this handbook is to offer recommendations concerning the needs of the disabled population as a whole. More specifically, it is concerned with the needs of people with a visual disability. In addressing their special requirements, designers, architects, planners and building managers will frequently improve the quality of the built environment for everyone.

So accustomed are people to tolerating poor design, that it is only when relevant faculties are diminished that some design shortcomings stand fully revealed. The overall objective should be to design any building or environment in such a way that all people - including people with a visual impairment - can move around as independently and freely as they would like. These fundamental issues need to be understood and incorporated from the very beginning of the design process.

14

'Architecture for the blind' redefined

The design recommendations in this book reflect the fact that the great majority of visually impaired people are not totally blind but have varying degrees of limited vision which they use as an aid to mobility.

However, if one looks at the research that has been conducted into an 'architecture for the blind' - a subject of much discussion from the mid-1960s to the mid-1970s - then lines of enquiry have focused on the needs of people born with blindness. Vanoli[1] summarises: 'The ability of many blind people to orient and locate themselves by using non-visual spatial information has led many to the conclusion that a blind person would benefit from an environment that complements and assists the blind person in this process.'

The notion of an 'architecture for the blind' embodied the recognition of a non-visual spatial conception of the world in which environments could be designed to offer non-visual clues, using touch, sound, aroma and kinaesthetic information derived from wind motion against body movement to aid mobility.

Mettler[2] comments on this process: 'Some sighted people exaggerate the extent to which blind people are sensitive to non-visual information, while others, lacking the skills to make substantial use of non-visual data, underestimate the potential value of this information.'

Mettler describes his experience of spatial location when vision is removed: 'Just as a sighted person explores the environment with the sensory apparatus available, so does a blind person, but in the latter case, primarily through

[1] Vanoli, D.V. Unsighted Barriers. Unpublished diploma thesis, 1972, available from RNIB Reference Library

[2] Mettler, R. Blindness and managing the environment. Journal of Visual Impairment and Blindness. Dec 1987 (10) P478-481

tactile, auditory, olfactory and kinaesthetic information[3]
gathering (supplemented by any residual vision). ...In time,
I found that remembered visual information gradually
diminished in significance... My working conception of
space was no longer built up by considering relative
positions of material objects as they appeared in my visual
field. Instead, it was built up by considering relative
positions of material objects separated by distances revealed
by movement as I detected varying tactile, auditory and
olfactory data. I then determined how objects were
arranged with respect to one another and my place among
them. Familiar strategies for making visual observations,
passive by comparison, gave way to strategies requiring a
greater level of active interaction with the environment[4].'

The idea of an 'architecture for the blind' has now largely
been rejected for the following reasons:

- architecture based on non-visual spatial concepts, that is
  completely tailored to the sensory needs, is not desirable or
  possible;

- architecture based on the orientation techniques of totally
  blind people caters for a very small minority of the visually
  impaired population, and it is almost impossible for
  architects and designers to conceptualise how each
  individual will utilise information from the environment;

- 'architecture for the blind' was subject to some backlash
  from blind and partially sighted people, who were against
  the provision of 'specialist' buildings when the majority of
  buildings would never be made more accessible.

Therefore we do not advocate an exclusive architecture for
blind people in this handbook. Instead we aim to explore a

---

[3] Mettler P478

[4] Mettler P477

16

whole series of inclusive design issues that should be considered in designing a built environment that will help everyone.

Previous notions of an 'architecture for the blind' were based on specialist facilities and buildings. The result would have been to enforce segregation and disempower people with a visual impairment. The view resonating through this book is that good architecture and design will empower and integrate all people.

However it must be said that this approach has been criticised by some. The first objection, expressed most strongly in the USA, is as follows: 'Environmental modifications advanced in the name of increasing the independence and integration of blind people, threaten to contribute to their dependence and isolation by reinforcing the belief that blind people are, by nature, inherently incompetent. The inescapable social consequence of this general belief is a reduction in opportunities for participation and success in most important areas of human endeavour[5].'

As the authors of this book, we reject this view. The argument for environmental accessibility should be seen in the context of equal opportunities. The prejudices and stereotypes arising from ignorance have to be confronted, and this must be part of the ongoing work of all involved in the disability movement.

The barriers posed by inaccessible environments, inadequate mobility training and lack of information, curtail the opportunity of many people with a visual impairment even to leave their own home.

[5] Mettler P481

A second objection has also been stated: 'No-one pretends that environmental modifications can realistically be put into place on any comprehensive scale... the result will be an archipelago of secure and convenient islands - mini institutions within the greater society. Thus independent access to the unmodified environment must ever remain something to which he or she dare not aspire[6].'

This theory of 'neo-institutionalisation' ignores the successes being achieved, albeit in small ways, by many organisations of disabled people in changing national building regulations, in campaigning hard for higher standards, and in ensuring that greater awareness is put into practice in improving the environment.

The problems posed by the construction of a built environment over hundreds of years will not be altered overnight, but the challenging of inappropriate, difficult and inaccessible environments is surely part of the process of challenging dependency. It shows that the inmates of the institution no longer accept the rules.

Some in this debate have argued that people with a visual impairment have accessed the environment per se without modifications in the past. These include not only American writers[7], but the influential Selwyn Goldsmith[8] in the UK, whose book has stood since the 1960s as the bible of design for disability.

However, research from RNIB's needs survey[9] does not vindicate this view: large numbers of people with a visual impairment appear isolated and trapped in their homes, with many dependent on sighted assistance for such tasks

[6] Mettler P481
[7] Vaughn, C. E. The Struggle of Blind People for Self Determination; Charles C. Thomas, Illinois, USA, 1993
[8] Goldsmith, S. Designing for the Disabled, McGraw-Hill, 1967
[9] Bruce, I., McKennell, A. and Walker, E.P.

18

as shopping. Modifying the environment will only be a partial answer to these problems, but it is an important issue which some disability activists have downgraded in the past.

The lessons of modification
In design terms, Mettler's 'classification of modifications' is a useful starting point. He identifies:

- modifications believed to introduce minimum, acceptable standards for safe access, which are tantamount to introducing physical access in practice;

- modifications to increase the margin of safety in existing access;

- modifications intended to render existing access more convenient.

In practice, however, it is difficult to put design modifications into these boxes. Some features such as audible crossing light beacons are seen by some as essential in locating crossing points and guiding decisions on when to cross, but less useful or not useful at all by others. It follows, therefore, that the provision of information, in a variety of forms, is an essential part of design.

Some modifications have also been counterproductive. A school teacher blinded as a child indicates how safety concerns can be taken too far: 'They had these ghastly gates at the top of stairs, and all they succeed in doing is hurting you in a nasty place[10].'

Any design change must be useful, practical, empowering or enabling, and the individual user is always the best judge

---

[10] Vanoli, P52

of any building modification. Therefore it is essential to listen to the comments of visually impaired users as part of the design process.

Learning from experience

Two or three years into the life of a new building, feedback should be sought from building users on the efficacy of the design. Unfortunately, however, it is not normal practice to invite the planners and designers back to sit alongside the building users and objectively review whether the building is actually meeting their requirements.

We believe this should become standard practice, even a contractual requirement (albeit one without penalties). How else can initial design and planning performance be improved unless property developers, architects and designers learn from the experience of those who occupy their buildings ?

Accessibility for all

Clearly, it is both commonsense and sound investment policy to design a building that is accessible to everyone, including those in wheelchairs or with sensory loss, whether required by legislation or not. This important objective should remain at the forefront of the building design strategy when considering future extensions.

Just as it is common practice for industrial buildings such as factories to be designed for possible future extension, so every building should adopt this approach. The built environment must be able to adapt to meet both the changing needs of society and the demands of the legislators. By building in flexibility through good future planning, it will be possible to utilise opportunities to

20

review the design and meet the needs of disabled people well into the life cycle of the building. With the help of the professional expertise of enlightened architects, designers and developers, it will be possible to create more inclusive design - a better architecture, not just for blind and partially sighted people but for everyone.

Chapter 2
The nature of visual loss

For architects, designers and developers to create buildings and environments that respond more effectively to the needs of visually impaired people, it is important that they should have some understanding of the nature of visual loss.

Only five per cent of those who are visually impaired have no sight at all. The remainder will have varying degrees of sight which will enable them to function visually to different degrees. The nature of visual handicap varies considerably between individuals. The overall picture is a complex, and in terms of design recommendations, sometimes a contradictory one, but generally the result of different eye conditions will lead to the following types of impairment:

- a limited field of vision, being unable to see the sides or up and down;

- some loss of central vision limiting the ability to see fine detail;

- gross shortsightedness, seeing the world as a continuous blur;

- uncontrollable oscillations of the eyeball leading to an inability to see objects clearly;

- night blindness, a sensitivity to light and a tendency to be dazzled by glare.

Types of visual impairment

In broad terms, visual impairment falls into two main groups, although in practice there is some degree of overlap between the two.

Loss of sharpness across the visual field

This is where the individual experiences a loss of acuity right across the visual field. The term visual field refers to everything that can be seen at a glance: when looking directly at an object we still see things above, below, and to the sides of that object, as well as other items sited beyond it. This loss of sharpness in the visual field will mean that the individual affected will see the world in the form of a degraded picture. The degree and severity of the condition will determine the visual quality of the image seen.

If the loss is small, it will render the individual's view of the world as slightly blurred with objects appearing a little unclear. In this case detail will begin to merge together into a 'definable with difficulty' image. As the eye condition increases in severity, the perceived image becomes progressively blurred and indistinct. As it does so, objects become less definable and will merge into an indeterminate whole. At this point the world will be seen as a series of splodges, blurs and indefinable shapes all coming together in a kaleidoscope of moving patterns and tones.

Areas of non-vision

The second type of visual loss produces areas of 'non vision' within the visual field. This loss in the visual field can be either in the central area, as in macula degeneration, peripheral, as in glaucoma or some types of retinitis pigmentosa, or it can be combinations of the two, producing a kind of patchy vision which is sometimes associated with retinal problems or diabetes.

A loss in the central area is the most common form of visual impairment among elderly people; over 60 per cent of those who are registered have this form of impairment. This type of loss will mean that the sufferer will find it more difficult to see detail and perform near-vision tasks such as reading, sewing, and recognising people. An accompanying loss of colour perception is likely and so difficulties may arise in detecting subtle variations in colour. However, peripheral vision - which even in a 'normal' eye is progressively more blurred towards the edges of the visual field - is seldom affected. This means that the individual's ability to move about and negotiate objects is less affected than might at first be thought.

Casual observation of someone with a central sight loss will reveal apparent contradictions in performance of everyday tasks. On the one hand the person appears to move around with relative ease and a good degree of safety and independence, even though he or she is unable to read notices or recognise friends in the street. Someone with sight loss will be able to see where objects are situated but will experience varying degrees of difficulty in determining exactly what they are.

Familiarity with an area plus life experience are also factors in this particular equation. In familiar places the sufferer will move about in a much more relaxed way than on unfamiliar terrain. This might seem obvious but what is less easy to understand is how that person uses their life experience to interpret their environment.

24

Normal sight
All the relevant detail is instantly visible and there would
be no problem negotiating the area.
The four examples opposite show how the same scene
would look with various eye disorders.

Cataract
The scene begins to blur, some key features begin to merge and the detail is drastically reduced; signs would be difficult to read.

Macular degeneration
No central vision makes wayfinding extremely difficult even though peripheral vision remains. Signs would be impossible to read.

Tunnel vision
A very small central part of the scene is visible giving no warning of hazards and making progress very slow.

Diabetic retinopathy
Patchy vision results in lack of sharpness across the visual field; the scene merges together making it almost impossible to see which way to travel.

As an example, imagine a street scene: The pavement stretches ahead into the distance and there is a high wall on the left. On the edge of the pavement there is a rectangular red 'something' that stands vertically. This 'something' is very blurred and the person with a central loss will not see the object as a whole when looking directly at it. The detail which normally helps to identify the object will be merged into its overall image giving little or no help. But life experience will quickly identify this red 'something' as a pillar box and the position of the slot into which the letter must be posted will be relatively easy to locate.

It must be borne in mind that wherever the eye is looking, the area of 'non vision' will follow. This will obscure detail and make it difficult to see the desired line of travel and whether any object lies in the way. However, it will be noticed that peripheral vision is not affected. By using a technique known as 'eccentric fixation' the line of travel/object can be placed outside the central spot and although detail will not be sharp, there will be sufficient information to identify whether the way is clear or not. In other words, the traveller with this type of vision must learn not to look at what he or she wants to see.

This eccentric fixation technique is one which is not easy to acquire, particularly in old age. After a lifetime of 'conditioning' in which the person has used central vision in order to see clearly what he/she is looking at, beginning to learn new techniques of seeing requires a high level of determination and motivation on the part of the person concerned.

It must be remembered that even with eccentric fixation the image perceived will not by anywhere near as sharp as previously experienced. At best, sufficient detail will be revealed to render the object more interesting or negotiable. It should also be pointed out that anyone with this condition will always have a central 'blank' area no matter how much he or she moves the eyes. Eccentric fixation merely moves the image perceived by the eye onto a better part of the retina away from the now damaged central part. Therefore, every time the eye moves, the central blank area moves also.

Glare problems

There are a number of eye conditions which are adversely affected by glare. The most common of these is cataract which is an opacity of the lens of the eye. The area affected and the degree of vision present will clearly be determined by the size and density of cataracts, and therefore the simulation is approximate at best. A sighted simulation of the effect cataract has on vision can be experienced when driving a car with a dirty windscreen into an evening sun. The low sun strikes the dirt on the windscreen causing light to scatter, producing a loss of detail and contrast. It is therefore very important that lighting, be it natural or artificial, is provided in such a way as to minimise the effect of glare.

The ageing process

A high proportion (16 per cent) of the population in the UK is over the age of 65, and this figure will increase in the foreseeable future. As people grow older the ability to see fine detail is diminished and the eyes have increasing difficulty in accommodating sudden changes of light or rapid re-focusing, such as when looking up from a task to a distant or near distant object.

This is in part due to physical changes in the structure of the eye which affects the lens, and other elements within the eyeball, as well as the muscles which surround it (see Appendix a: How the eye works).

Changes in the transparency and thickness of the lens will inhibit the passage of light. In addition to this the muscles of the eye become weak, leading to focusing difficulties and a reduced pupil size, which in turn limits the amount of light reaching the retina still further.

The implication for this is clear to see. Older people need more light. In fact, roughly twice the amount of light is needed at the age of 60 than at 40. It is also thought that, generally speaking, someone with a visual impairment will need between 50 per cent and 100 per cent more light than their sighted counterparts, and in some cases even more.

The most common aid used by people with poor sight to facilitate their mobility is another person's assistance. A sighted guide will normally walk by the side but slightly ahead, of the person with a visual impairment who will hold their upper arm with one hand. This form of guidance obviously has implications in terms of door widths, corridor widths and so on.

The second common aid used by people with poor sight to facilitate their mobility is a white cane. There are a host of different types, but the most familiar is the one used to scan the ground in front of the person. This scanning takes the form of sweeping the cane in an arc from one side to the other to just over the width of the body. This technique only locates low level items in the immediate vicinity.

Overhanging objects above approximately 300mm will be missed by the cane.

A visually impaired person may have a guide dog to assist them with their mobility. Whilst there are approximately 4,250 guide dog owners at the present time in the UK, this might increase substantially in the future.

Guide dogs are also limited in their ability to detect overhanging objects. If collisions and possible serious injury are to be avoided, then hanging and/or projecting hazards must be indicated or protected at ground level or, better still, eliminated altogether.

Working with a dog again raises issues with regard to door widths, and so on. A person with a guide dog generally requires more width than a wheelchair, and if shopping or other baggage is being carried, ample width is required for easy passage.

If pathways are to be easily identified with peripheral vision (which is blurred in everyone) they must be differentiated from adjacent walls. Any objects situated on them will need to stand out so that they can be recognised as an obstruction. Items such as notices or signs may be seen as little more than a rectangular shape on the wall or suspended from the ceiling, with the print perceived as a series of wavy lines and swirls.

Generally speaking the person with a central loss will view objects in gross terms, all details and textures merging together into an indefinable mass; nevertheless they will still be 'seen' and dealt with in the appropriate way provided they contrast with the background against which they are seen.

Tunnel vision

The type of visual loss commonly known as 'tunnel vision' causes the sufferer to lose all, or most, of their peripheral vision whilst retaining normal acuity in a reduced central spot. 'Tunnel vision' is something of a misnomer as it implies that the person sees a reduced area of the scene surrounded by an area of blackness. This is not the case, even if the loss of peripheral vision is total. The visible area will be reduced, but there will be no surrounding blackness.

In severe cases of tunnel vision it may be necessary for the individual to 'scan' the area in order to locate the visual information which is being sought. This scanning technique must be repeated with each step the person takes to ensure that relevant information is gained at the last second and that the way ahead is clear.

One of the difficulties with this type of visual loss is that mobile objects at the side suddenly come into view, leaving little time to avoid a collision. Also low objects may remain undetected, particularly when the sufferer is focused on his/her destination. It is easy for someone walking across a crowded room to fall over low objects such as furniture outside the field of view.

Peripheral vision also enables us to see in the dark, and so severe peripheral loss diminishes this ability, which in turn will affect the person's mobility in variable lighting conditions. There are many apparent contradictions in this condition. People with peripheral loss may grope about in the dark and will be almost totally blind, but if lighting conditions are 'just right' then they may be able to move around with relative ease. They may well be able to read the smallest print in a newspaper, or spot a needle on the carpet whilst sitting in an armchair, but when moving about start to collide with objects.

A combination of visual loss

In some eye conditions the effect on vision is, or can be, a combination of all these factors. In other words, the person can experience a degree of loss in the central field and also various losses within the peripheral area, producing a 'patchy' type of vision.   The position and size of this 'patchiness' will determine how the individual sees the world and the density of these patches will affect the amount of detail which becomes visible. People with this condition will see the world differently, depending on the position and size of the blank areas.

When someone incurs damage to the optic pathways between the back of the eye and the visual cortex, the same side of the visual field is affected in both eyes and, in many cases, the whole of one side of the visual field is lost. From the mobility point of view, the biggest problem is the loss of peripheral vision on the side which is affected, with the inevitable result that collisions are likely to occur with both stationary and mobile objects, and people situated on that particular side. Reading signs and notices may also be difficult (see Chapter 8).

Implications for building design

It will be apparent from the above that all this has significant implications for the building and interior design process.

A design checklist is shown on the next page.

32

Design checklist

Layout

Forming a clear mental picture of a building and its surroundings is made much easier if there is a simple, logical layout. Once formed, this mental picture is also more easily memorised for the future when the building design is straightforward and rational.

To a certain extent logical planning can be helpful in helping people to anticipate probable locations: stairs situated next to lifts, for example, or male and female toilets located next to one another.

More detailed issues about building layout are dealt with later in this book.

Visibility

If the key features of a building are visually accentuated this can be very helpful to visually impaired people. For example, columns in circulation areas should be coloured to stand out from the background, not merge in with it.

The same logic of visibility and differentiation should be applied to a whole range of building features - handrails, stair nosings, doors, glass panels, light switches and so on. Colour and tone contrasts are the most effective means of improving visibility, with tone contrast usually the more effective. A conventionally pleasing co-ordinated colour scheme can usually be significantly enhanced with good tonal contrast.

Lighting

Good lighting is vitally important not only to visually impaired people but to all building users. Adequate lighting levels, well-designed lights and proper positioning are all necessary if other aids to visibility are not to be compromised by glare, dazzle and the unwelcome optical illusions caused by heavy shadows.

These three general areas of concern - layout, visibility and lighting - must form the basis of any environment that is to be accessible and welcoming to everybody. The next section of this book expands upon these and other issues that contribute to the concept of inclusive building design.

Design Practicalities

This section provides a reference guide to the design practicalities involved in creating buildings and environments which can be a good experience for everyone, including visually impaired people.

From the siting of the building, its approachways, surroundings and entrance, to the fixtures, fittings and finishes of the interior, lighting, signing and design of specific types of facility, a range of key issues are raised and appropriate solutions presented.

Basic principles followed in this section are:

providing simple lay-out, which is logical and, therefore, memorable;

use of colour and tone contrast to raise visibility;

adequate and evenly distributed lighting;

careful use of touch, sound, fragrance and air movement techniques;

highly visible, tactile embossed and concise signs.

Chapter 3

Site, street and surroundings

Influencing site location

In practice the siting of a new building or group of buildings will often have been predetermined by the developer and planner. In cases where the architect is able to exercise influence, it is important to take into account the needs of all the building users when deciding how to make best use of the site whilst achieving the optimum shape and orientation to the structure. Ideally, the developer or planner will already have given serious thought to these issues; if not, the architect should ensure that they are fully explored at the earliest possible stage.

Wherever practical, sites should be level and close to all amenities. Routes to nearby amenities such as shops, leisure facilities, public transport systems and housing should be carefully considered to make access direct and safe. It should be appreciated that disabled people rely heavily on public transport. Where changes in level are unavoidable, ramps should be used whenever possible. The necessity to cross busy roads or negotiate cluttered areas should be kept to an absolute minimum.

The whole site should be made accessible to people with a wide range of disabilities. Sites that manage to achieve this are user-friendly for everyone, including elderly people and those with prams or buggies. It is always worth remembering that the best integrated schemes can be spoilt by lack of attention to detail: a caretaker's house with steps

Hazard warning paving (corduroy): a pattern of half rod shaped bars to give warning of a hazard which requires caution eg at the top and bottom of a flight of stairs.

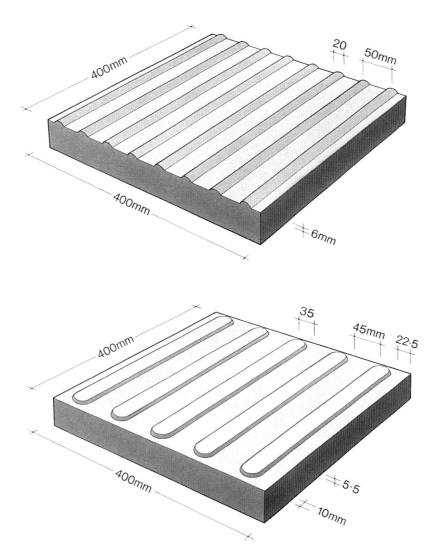

Directional guidance paving: round ended bars which are used to guide visually impaired pedestrians through a large, open space eg a pedestrian precinct or a town square. The bars are laid in the direction of travel and turned at corners to give warning of a change of direction.

Modified blister paving: small, regular flat topped domes alert pedestrians to a safe crossing (zebra or pelican) and warn them that there is no kerb at the crossing where it has been dropped to assist wheelchair users and others.

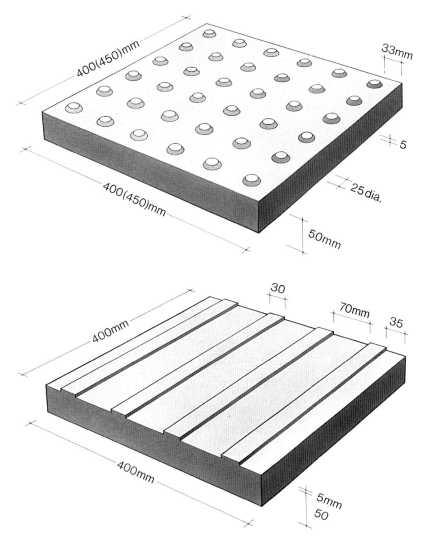

Cycleway paving: the bar pattern is laid on shared pedestrian / cycle routes which are not segregated by level. The paving is laid transverse to denote pedestrian use, and longitudinal to denote cycle path.

40

to the door, for example, or large spaces with no mobility aids for visually impaired people, can undo much good work in other areas.

Pathways and footways

The surfacing on footways approaching or surrounding the building should be firm, even, and level; it must not become slippery when wet. The crossfall should not exceed 2.5 per cent because an excessive crossfall or camber may cause a blind person to deviate from the correct route. Where a footway is paved with slabs, the gap between adjacent slabs should not exceed 5mm, and the vertical deviation should be kept to a minimum, not exceeding 10mm.

The edge of the footway should be clearly defined, either by a kerb or by a distinct change of texture, such as grass or gravel. Incidentally, gravel footpaths are not a good idea since they are virtually unusable by people in wheelchairs or those with ambulatory problems. If it is necessary to define the edge of a footpath by an upstand, it should have a minimum height of 50mm when accompanied by a handrail, although 100mm is preferable. A 100mm high upstand would not necessarily require a handrail above it, unless the ground falls away steeply.

Handrails can be a very effective way of providing additional guidance to visually impaired people. These should be colour-contrasted with the background against which they will be seen. They should be smooth and comfortable to the touch. Sharp edges and corners should be avoided. Handrails should also accord with the specification set out in Building Regulations Part M.

Where footpaths lie on a significant gradient, horizontal resting places should be provided at frequent intervals. Research has indicated that 50m is the maximum distance that can be comfortably covered at a stretch by many people, particularly those who are elderly or with ambulatory difficulties. Resting places on a level surface might therefore be introduced at slightly shorter intervals - say 30m.

Drainage grilles should be offset from pedestrian route and set flush with the surrounding surface. The gap between grille bars should not exceed 13mm, and bars should be set at right-angles to the direction of travel, so that they do not present a potential trap for the tip of a long cane or the wheel of a pram.

Street-level aids
There are a number of design issues to consider in relation to the approachways to the building and its surroundings.

Tactile surfaces: The ground surface or floor covering has a significant effect on the appearance of an area and it can also be a useful source of information. A number of different profiles have been developed, each of which has a specific meaning, and they are available in a variety of materials and colours providing flexibility and choice. However, it should be emphasised that the integrity of the profile must be maintained and the surface must be used in the correct application.

The most commonly used pattern is the modified blister, which should be used externally at a dropped kerb or raised road surface to indicate the edge of the footway and the start of the carriageway.

Hazard warning patterns (corduroy), a half-rod shaped profile, are now required by Building Regulations Part M at the

Contrast paving to denote vehicle crossover.

Tactile paving to indicate
a zebra crossing.

Colour and texture
changes alert people to the
difference between
footway and carriageway.

Modified blister paving indicates the absence of a kerb at a speed control table.

Bad practice crossing. T shaped configuration indicates that this is a controlled zebra crossing but there are no lights or crossing.

44

A dark bollard on light paving highlights the bollard form for visually impaired people. The bollard also has a light coloured top and collar to further enhance its presence.

Good example of bollards showing maximum contrast marking against a pale coloured pavement.

Well lit bollards are essential at night.

top of an external flight of steps and should also be used at the top and bottom of internal stairs.

A flat-topped, ribbed profile denotes a guidance path. This pattern has been used successfully in shopping precincts, and pedestrian precincts.

The increased use of bicycles and the need to keep cyclists separate from other road users has stimulated the interest in shared facilities - a cycle track running parallel, and on the same level as, a footpath. Separation of the two is achieved by the use of the fourth pattern, a continuous bar, laid transversely (pedestrians) and longitudinally (cyclists), with a raised dividing line between the track and footpath.

Crossovers: Wherever practical, a crossover should be set flush with the pavement, whilst being distinguished from it by a different texture and different colour surfacing. There is normally no need to indicate the crossover by tactile paving. However, if it is located at a busy entrance to premises like a garage, hospital, or factory, then other considerations arise. It may, for example, be necessary to treat the crossover as if it were a side road by providing a dropped kerb and tactile paving.

Road crossing: Wherever a footway crosses a traffic route, there should be a conventional 150-200mm kerb. If a dropped kerb is necessary for the benefit of other pedestrians, it must be clearly indicated by tactile paving - wherever there is a dropped kerb, there must be tactile paving.

Where there is heavy traffic and pedestrian flow, it may be necessary to provide a controlled zebra or pelican type of crossing. Here, the disposition of tactile paving is slightly different. If a traffic control light is used, as on a pelican crossing, the light should be supplemented by a green man, audible indicator and tactile rotating knob to assist those who are visually and hearing impaired.

Traffic calming features: Some currently fashionable techniques for reducing traffic speed pose particular problems to visually impaired pedestrians. The best indicator to a blind person that they have reached the edge of the pavement, and are about to step onto the road, is the conventional kerb. If that is removed by raising the surface of the road, or carriageway to the same level of the pavement, the effect can be confusing. Then the change of footway into carriageway must be indicated by appropriate tactile paving. The message should also be reinforced by providing a different colour and texture of paving between the footway and the carriageway surface.

Bollards: Bollards are a fairly common feature of pedestrian areas, providing a cheap and effective way of separating traffic and pedestrians. However, when badly designed or poorly positioned, they are potentially perhaps the most serious street hazard. A knee-high, natural coloured concrete bollard can cause severe injury to an unsuspecting pedestrian.

Bollards should be a minimum of 1m in height, and colour contrasted with the background against which they are seen - for example, a black bollard against light paving or concrete. There should also be a colour contrasted band around the neck of the bollard as a further aid to visibility. The bollard should not have any ornamental features projecting horizontally, and under no circumstances should adjacent bollards be linked with chain or rope.

48

The ramps shown here are bad examples. These present a hazard to everyone, not just visually impaired people, because there is a stepped change in gradient in the line of travel and no handrail to grasp or lower tapping rail.

If the approachway to the building is not level and ramps are used, these should provide a gentle, sloping gradient - preferably with handrails on both sides - in the good examples shown here.

50

Street furniture: Street furniture such as lighting columns, signposts, litter bins, seating and so on, are necessary and desirable features. However, once again, if they are not properly designed and positioned, they can be potential obstructions and hazards. They should be positioned out of the line of pedestrian travel, off (but adjacent to) the footway and effectively highlighted with colour and tone contrasting. For example, a signpost painted black to contrast with a light paved background should also have a white or light coloured band around it at eye level. This band should be 150mm deep with its bottom edge at between 1.4 and 1.6m above ground level.

In some cases it may be necessary to have a low level sign or notice board, such as near the entrance to a park. Sometimes such a sign is supported on two vertical poles, set far enough apart for an unsuspecting pedestrian, or a child, to walk between the poles and collide with the notice board. This can be prevented by the provision of a low level rail between the posts, which should also be suitably colour contrasted to make them easier to detect. It is important that this low rail is no higher than 250mm above ground level. This will also prevent a guide dog from walking between the posts. In addition, the extension of the sign beyond the vertical post on either side should not exceed 150mm, to prevent a pedestrian walking into it.

Benches and seats should be offset from the pedestrian route and colour contrasted so that they are clearly visible against their background. A light colour is helpful when the background is of dark vegetation. Litter bins, if attached to lamp posts or signposts, should be positioned facing the direction of travel. If they are free-standing, they should be continuous to ground level. A pedestal mounted basket which overhangs its support, could easily remain undetected by a white cane user and cause injury at hip or waist level. Litter bins should contrast with the background against which they will be seen and made with materials that will not cause injury if the litter bin itself is damaged. Sharp corners and edges which could trap fingers or tear clothing, should be avoided.

Vegetation

Vegetation can add enormously to both the attractiveness of an open space, and also the orientation of visually impaired people, if appropriately chosen and positioned. Trees and bushes should be positioned so that they do not present too much of a maintenance problem by overgrowing footpaths. A branch overhanging a footpath can cause serious injury. There should be constant maintenance or a policy of planting the vegetation well back from the edge of the footway.

Falling leaves, cones, nuts and so on, can all present particular problems to disabled people, and particularly those who are elderly, as the surface may become slippery, or uncomfortable to walk on.

On the positive side, many plants can act as useful landmarks and, therefore, aids to orientation. This may be because the plant has a particular fragrance, colour, or very distinctive shape.

Open spaces

Large open spaces, as found in shopping precincts or pedestrianised areas, can cause particular wayfinding problems to visually impaired people. Unless there are sufficient landmarks available, following a particular route can be extremely difficult, if not impossible. The strategic

Overhanging trees and foliage and unmarked road works
are typical of the hazards that threaten the safety of
visually impaired people and others. They are frequently
overlooked by the responsible authorities.

Well marked road works include warning signs in advance of the hazard as well as double rails and lights. An auditory warning would also be advantageous.

54

use of textures and colours can be very useful for identifying desired routes across open spaces as well as for defining areas which have different functions, for example rest areas, play areas and so on. Distinct profiles have been developed to indicate a guide path and 'proceed with caution' or 'hazard ahead' warnings.

Approachways

If the approach to the building cannot be level, there should be a gentle gradient, preferably not exceeding 1 in 20. If ramps are used, there should be a handrail on both sides, and there should be a ground level upstand, kerb or tapping rail. The upstand at the edge of a ramp should be a minimum height of 100mm, and no more than 200mm. A tapping rail, or kicking rail, should be positioned so that its top edge is no higher than 200mm above ground level.

If steps are provided in addition to a ramp, they should also be properly equipped with handrails on both sides and with a highlighted or colour contrasted nosing extending the full width of each and every step. In the case of a strip, it should be as close to the edge of the step as possible and should provide effective colour contrast so that the edge of the step is clearly visible in all lighting and weather conditions. Nosings should be between 50 and 65mm in depth on both the tread and riser and the material used should sit flush with the tread and riser.

Although there should be a tactile warning at the top and bottom of the stairs or steps, it should not normally be used at the top and bottom of ramps. Dimensions for ramps, steps and handrails, are given in Chapter 5.

Exterior design

Entrances

Just as the building itself must be identifiable - perhaps by its distinctive shape, the landscaping around it, effective signing or perhaps even its use of tactile indicators - so should the entrance.

Unfortunately there are too many examples of buildings with single glass panel doors which are indistinguishable from similar fixed panels stretching out in both directions. The entrance to a building is important and its design should make it recognisable and inviting.

Although much progress has been made since the days when every imposing house or public building could only be entered by climbing half a dozen scrubbed stone steps, the importance of a flat and level entrance approach is still overlooked. Steps are a difficult and sometimes dangerous hazard for people with a visual impairment. Every effort should be made to improve on the minimum requirements spelt out in Building Regulations Part M.

Entrance canopies

Where an external canopy is used over an entrance, either as protection or as a feature, any supporting columns must not present an obstruction on the entrance approach. Columns and canopy may then be used positively to help identify the entrance. The area underneath the canopy should be adequately illuminated during the hours of darkness.

External doors

Building Regulations now require external doors to be a minimum of 800mm wide. Although this is adequate for the free passage of wheelchairs, it is not wide enough to allow free passage of a blind person with a guide dog, or a blind person plus a sighted companion. The width required for a blind person plus guide dog is 1.1m and for a blind person plus a sighted escort is 1.2m. Every effort should therefore be made to consider 1.2m the minimum acceptable width for external doors.

Type of door

The choice of door type is most important. Automatic sliding doors are strongly recommended as this type provides the least barrier to disabled people or those who are frail and elderly, as well as to those walking with children, carrying luggage, or pushing a pram.

Automatic hinged doors are potentially dangerous unless the leading edge is protected so that an unsuspecting person cannot walk into it. This can be achieved with double doors working in unison, but then any environmental control benefits are virtually eliminated.

Where side-hung doors are used, care must be taken to ensure that the spring pressure is sufficient to keep the door closed without making it difficult to open. (Door closure springs should be set so that the maximum force required to open the door does not exceed 15 Newtons.)

Door furniture should be conveniently positioned with a handle of the lever type (D or L-shaped type if the door is opened by pulling/pushing).

The revolving door is a difficult door for all - particularly so for people with a visual impairment. Anyone who doubts this should just stand by the entrance to a supermarket or hotel where there is a revolving door and adjacent side-hung door and watch the choices people make. The revolving door is likely to be used by children who are having fun and by people who are fit, able and not carrying anything with them. Everybody else will use the adjacent side-hung door or automatic door, unless it is inaccessible or obscure.

Even the large revolving doors now coming into fashion are by no means easy to negotiate with a pram, luggage or shopping trolley let alone with a guide dog or a sighted escort. It is true that revolving doors offer a simple and space-saving way of achieving environmental control. However two pairs of automatic sliding doors with a minimum space between them of 1.5m provide the best access, as well as acceptable control of heating, air-conditioning and ventilation. They can also be set to an open or fail-safe position in the event of an emergency.

Further development of very large powered revolving doors may provide an answer to both the problems of free, independent, unrestricted access and environmental control. However, this type of door remains relatively untested and needs further refinement before it can be recommended.

The threshold in doorways should be flush. If an upstand or weather bar is unavoidable, its height should be restricted to 15mm maximum and it should have chamfered edges to reduce the risk of tripping.

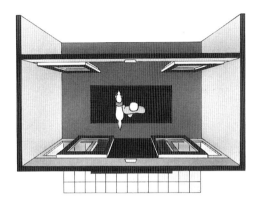

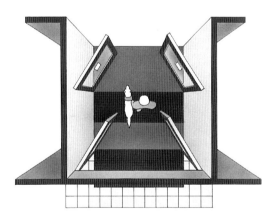

External doors should be wide enough
to accommodate a visually impaired
person with a guide dog and helper.
A minimum width of 1.2m is
recommended.

This unprotected, free-standing, external staircase is a major hazard. It would be safer if it was enclosed or had planting at its base to stop people from running into it.

An entrance which suffers from dazzling reflections from the canopy lights, has no protection on the edges of the manual doors and an inadequate warning strip.

Well defined entrance with good colour contrast between doors, frames and warning strip.

External staircases need handrails, stair nosings and adequate illumination if they are to be safe.

60

It is most important to ensure that where ramped access is provided in addition to steps, the two routes are perceived to be of equal importance. Those people who have no option but to use the ramp should not be directed to a secondary entrance.

Distinguishing the door position

The door should be distinguishable from adjacent walls or panels by the use of colour contrasting, lighting and by colour and textural differences in floor finishes. Doormats inside and outside the building can be a useful aid, but care must be taken that they are not trip hazards, and, if they are set in a well, that they should not become a trap for the unsuspecting wheelchair user.

Glazed doors and side panels should be highlighted with prominent signs, logos, emblems or decorative features at eye level. Anything smaller than a 150mm square set in a standard glass panel is unlikely to be large enough adequately to signal the presence of the glass.

The material or pattern used to highlight the presence of glass should be at a height of between 1.4 and 1.6m above ground level. It is helpful to repeat this at a lower level too: approximately 850mm to 1m above ground level, and again with a 150mm skirting across the bottom of the glass panel. Whatever highlighting technique is used it must be effective from both inside or outside the building and under any lighting conditions.

Door furniture

Door furniture should be positioned logically and colour contrasted with the door or door frame. Door handles on external doors should be positioned approximately

1 to 1.25m above ground level, and at a consistent height throughout any given building.

External staircases

A building's external staircase should be constructed to the same standards as are required for internal stairs. That is to say the steps should be uniform, the treads not less than 280mm and the riser not greater than 150mm. There should also be a handrail on each side and the edge of each step should be highlighted with a nosing. A tactile warning surface should be incorporated at the top of the stairs. (It is now a requirement of Building Regulations Part M that a tactile warning surface is used at the top of external stairs.)

The staircase should be adequately and uniformly illuminated during the day - and similarly lit at night if it is likely to be used then.

The underside of stairs should be enclosed or protected in order to prevent anyone walking underneath them from receiving a head injury on the sloping underside of the structure. Open riser stairs should not be used.

Interior design

Layout

The building layout should be logical. The reception area should be close to the entrance to the building. Other essential services, such as toilets, lifts, staircases, should all be grouped together in that area, rather than dispersed to remote parts of the building. Wherever possible doorways to essential services should be off a central circulating area or adjacent corridors. There should be level access throughout each individual floor. Consideration should be given to how the building could be extended or altered if requirements change in the future.

Circulation areas

Within the constraints of the building design, every effort should be made to ensure that internal support columns and pillars are not positioned in interior circulation areas where they will obstruct free movement. If this is unavoidable, the obstruction they represent needs to be flagged with decorative treatment or dealt with by means of protective measures. In certain cases, a virtue can be made out of a necessity by deploying such columns and pillars as orientation landmarks.

Internal doors

Ideally internal doors should open automatically, but in practice this cannot always be justified. More probably they will be side hung.

Building Regulations Part M currently require that internal doors should be a minimum of 750mm width. As discussed in the external doors section, this is inadequate for visually impaired people and a minimum width of 800mm - preferably 1m - is strongly recommended.

In many cases these widths may only be achieved by using a pair of side hung doors. In such cases, should one door leaf be wider than the other, consistency becomes important: the wider leaf should always be on the same side in consecutive sets of doors.

Internal doors should also have a vision panel so that people in wheelchairs can see - and be seen - through the glass. If the doors are fully or largely glazed, the glazing must be adequately highlighted to prevent accidental collision.

Door furniture should be colour contrasted and logically positioned. L-shaped, D-shaped or lever handles are preferred. The open end of a lever handle should always be turned in towards the door, to reduce its chance of becoming caught in an open sleeve. Doors should never open outwards onto corridors, passages or hallways.

Interior staircases
The hazard warning surface now required to be used at the top of external stairs should be applied to interior staircases where it can be used at both top and bottom.

Particular care should be taken during the design of the building envelope to ensure that interior stairs are not a continuation of the normal line of pedestrian travel along the corridor or landing. It is much safer if a person wishing to descend or ascend a staircase has to make a conscious 90 degree change of direction.

Stairs should be straight wherever possible. If a change of direction is necessary, this should be achieved by use of a half-landing rather than by two or three steps angled to achieve a 90 degree bend. Spiral staircases are best avoided. They can cause problems of disorientation for visually impaired people, particularly if they cover more than one change of floor level.

The most effective way of highlighting the edge of a step is by the provision of a nosing on every step. The same rules apply in terms of uniformity of nosing and handrails as for exterior staircases. Highly reflective interior nosing materials such as bright stainless steel or polished brass are best avoided as the glare reflection can cause disorientation to people with poor eyesight.

Handrails should be positioned at a height of 1m above the surface of the landing and 900mm above the pitch line of a flight of stairs, beginning and ending with a horizontal section at least 300mm beyond the edge of the top or bottom of the step. The end of the handrail should be turned in towards the wall or otherwise adequately end-stopped.

The cross section of the handrail should be between 45 and 50mm in diameter and the handrail should be supported on brackets which do not obstruct continuous hand contact with the handrail. Should handrails continue from the stair onto the corridor of lobby wall, it is suggested that buttons be inserted in the handrail at the top of stairs, to indicate floor level.

The underside of the staircase should be enclosed to prevent

The first two illustrations are good examples of glazed doors which should be highlighted with patterns, decals or corporate logos to prevent accidental collision. The third example would present a hazard because it has no contrast to the edge of the door and no warning strip on the glass.

Hazardous spiral staircase in confined space with no warning or contrast marking.

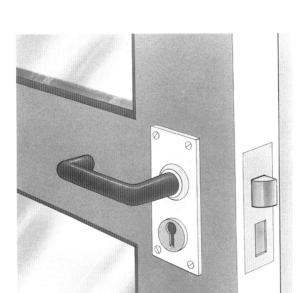

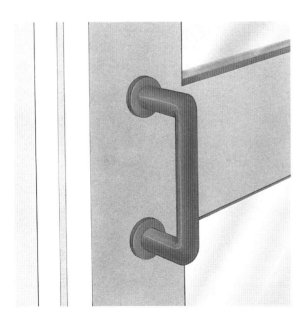

L-shaped, D-shaped and lever handles are easier to use than spherical or highly decorated knobs.

68

accidents caused by passing beneath the angled support structure of the stairs. Normally in a domestic or commercial building this space provides a useful storage area if boxed in. But some retail, entertainment or leisure environments leave the space open. Discreet use of furniture and/or decorations such as screens or plants can make such areas attractive, and also safe.

Corridors and hallways

Corridors should be left unobstructed with fire extinguishers and radiators recessed. However, large hallways or long corridors can be very disconcerting for visually impaired people who need clues to orientate themselves. It is, therefore, very important to provide appropriate information to enable them to interpret correctly the environment and act accordingly.

In the past, rails along the walls of corridors and hallways were thought to be all that was required to enable people with little or no sight to negotiate the area. In more recent times, designers have become much more enlightened, and while handrails are still a useful and sometimes vital feature, they play a relatively minor role. When provided, they should do considerably more than simply maintain a line of travel: they can be made to convey a great deal of additional information about the surrounding physical environment.

For example, the use of different materials in their construction could convey helpful information like 'stairs are being approached' or 'there is a junction opposite'. Texture changes and raised symbols can also be incorporated to provide additional information useful to totally blind people. Handrails may also provide support and a sense of psychological comfort to older people or those with other disabilities.

In general, corridors and halls should be kept as short as possible to facilitate orientation for all users. Everyone needs certain landmarks to identify where they are. These may be one or a combination of such features as visible clues, tactile indicators, sounds, fragrances or changes of air movement.

The end wall of a corridor needs to be highlighted. This can be achieved, for example, by good colour and tone contrast between the walls and floor coverings. If necessary, a change of direction within a corridor should be at 90 degrees: curved corridors and oblique angles are to be avoided whenever possible.

In long corridors, consideration should be given to the provision of resting places and perhaps a dado rail to provide support for those who need it. Where long corridors are unavoidable, regulations state that they must be broken up by the use of firedoors. These firedoors have to conform to the required legal standards, but additionally, for the benefit of visually impaired people, they should all be hung the same way.

Where doors of differing widths are used, the wider door should always be on the same side throughout the length of the corridor. Doors that are held open by electronically linked magnetic catches make passage easier for everyone, providing that the leading edges of the doors are held flat against adjacent walls. The recommended minimum width for passages or corridors in residential use is 1.2m. Doors which open outwards into corridor or circulation areas must be fitted with door closers or rising butt hinges.

A hazard warning pattern should be positioned
at the top and bottom of all interior staircases.

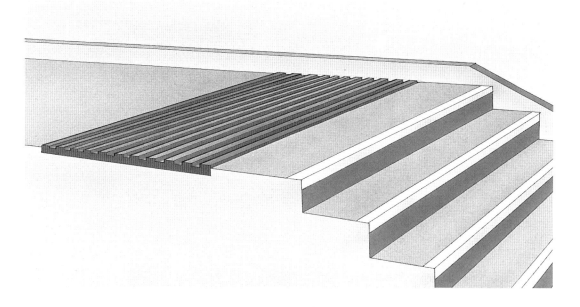

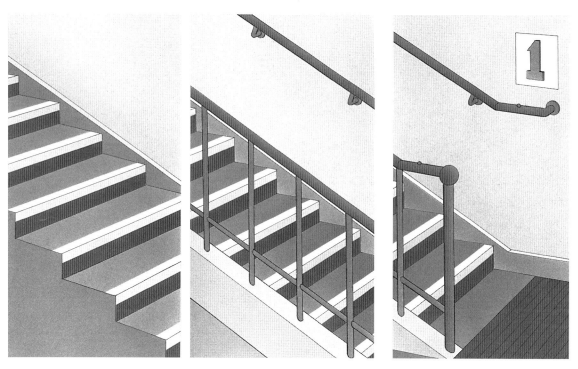

The tread should be highlighted with high visibility nosing (left).
Handrails should be 900mm above the pitch line (centre) and should
extend horizontally at least 300mm beyond the edge of the top and
bottom step (right).

Prominent floor numbers and handrails which return to the wall, to denote
the top or bottom of the stairs, help visually disabled people negotiate
stairs. Tactile bumps on the handrail at the top and the bottom of staircases
can be used to indicate floor level, eg: two bumps for the second floor and
so on. These bumps additionally warn of the presence of a staircase.

Windows positioned at the end of corridors or passageways can cause glare problems which may be reduced by using tinted glass, anti-glare treatment or some form of blind. South facing windows are notorious while east or west facing ones can be particularly susceptible to low sunlight in mornings or evenings.

Windows

Glare from windows in the line of travel poses a recurring problem. As with corridors, windows at the top and bottom of staircases and on half landings require careful measures to reduce glare. A window positioned at the top of a flight of stairs and facing south-west may cause an accident if low evening sunlight dazzles someone using the stairs. Adjustable blinds should be fitted to these windows.

This problem may be less serious when windows are north facing but here too some glare and a sense of discomfort may add to disorientation. The use of blinds, curtains or shutters will help.

Windows at ground floor or raised walkway levels, should not open outwards onto a pedestrian route where they may cause accidents by people walking into them.

When full-length or picture windows are installed, it is important to make sure that an unsuspecting person does not walk into the glass, believing the window to be open or even failing to notice it at all. One solution may be to highlight the glass with a decorative or informative sign. Any highlighted area must be of sufficient size to attract attention. On a 2m x 1m panel, an acceptable surface area of highlighting might be a 150mm x 150mm square or perhaps a logo of a similar surface area.

Any material used for highlighting should be opaque or near-opaque. It should also be colour contrasted with the background against which it is seen - not always an easy task to achieve with a single tone material since different lighting conditions may make different visibility demands. Here a two-tone material is likely to provide the best solution.

Floor covering

Floor coverings should be of a matt finish - such as carpet or matt vinyl - which will not cause reflections from windows or light fittings. Shiny floor surfaces create reflections of any objects or fittings in the area. This creates additional visual confusion and makes it more difficult for visually impaired people to safely negotiate the space. High gloss floors feel slippery, even if they are not. Particularly disturbing are high gloss floors which reflect the movement of other people, or - as can be found in one major airport terminal - the image of overhead revolving ventilators.

Floor finishes should contrast with the walls so that the boundary of the floor is clearly visible. Where floor coverings are of a similar hue to wall finishes, it is important that the skirting board is picked out in a dark colour to ensure that it is easy for the visually impaired person to locate where the floor ends and the wall begins.

Where changes in level occur within an area, such as a step or steps along a corridor, the leading edge of these steps should be clearly marked with a contrasting line. If the floor is carpeted, this can be achieved by the use of white PVC or similar nosing to the step. The carpet must be flush with the nosing to minimise the risk of people catching heels or toes on the nosing.

In the poorly designed corridor (below), doors, radiators and fire extinguishers are potential hazards.

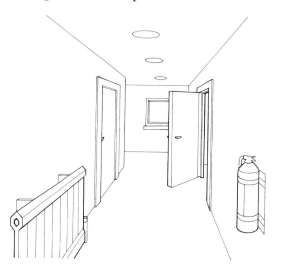

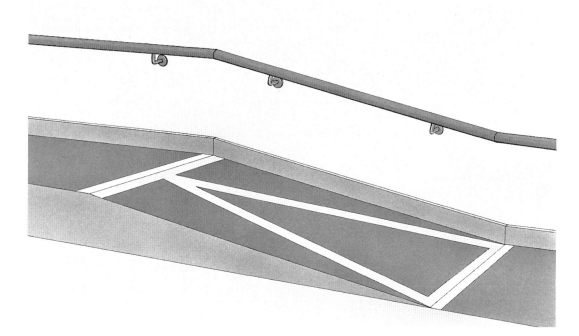

A triangle symbol on an internal ramp indicates both its presence and the direction of the incline.

The same corridor as top left but well designed. Fire extinguishers and radiators are recessed and a hand rail provides a line of travel and a warning of door entrances.

Where short ramps occur, these also need to be highlighted. One way of doing this might be to have a line across the corridor at the top and bottom of the ramp, together with two diagonal lines from the base of the ramp to the mid-point of the top. This will not only make the ramp more visible, but also give an indication as to the direction the ramp is sloping.

Changes in floor textures can help people to identify different locations and they can also be used to indicate a possible source of danger. For example, an upstairs corridor which is carpeted could have a change in floor finish inserted in front of the fire exit door to an external staircase.

In very large areas, 'walkways' can be created by the use of a floor surfacing with different tactile and colour-contrasting characteristics. Department stores, hotels, offices, and museums can use this principle. If the design is executed carefully, it can be aesthetically pleasing as well as helpful to visually impaired people. Finally, the change from a solid to a suspended floor is another technique that can be used to provide information.

Reception areas
It is important that reception desks are strategically placed, clearly signed and easily identifiable by their general surrounding. This can be achieved by using materials that provide good colour and tonal contrast with the immediate surroundings. Well positioned lighting which illuminates the receptionist and the desk top without creating glare will also help. Furthermore the desk top should not have a reflective surface.

High gloss floor finishes are to be avoided because by reflecting both natural and artificial light they can also distort environmental images to an unrecognisable degree. Any signs or information boards in the reception area should be designed with reference to the detailed guidance set out in Chapter 10.

A high level of background noise is confusing, distressing and disorientating to some disabled people. For this reason reception area acoustics should be carefully planned and controlled.

Adjoining areas and services, such as staircases, lifts, toilets and entrances to office suites, need to be clearly identifiable. Good design practice, including the use of colour and tone contrast for doorways, is vital.

It is possible to provide a simple layout of any premises in the form of a combined tactile/visual map. These are available through RNIB or commercial suppliers.

Public waiting areas

Large rooms can be a problem in terms of orientation. With careful thought and planning, large areas can be broken down into smaller units by varying elements such as light fittings, furniture or floor coverings in different parts of the space.

For example, in a retail outlet it might be appropriate for sales areas to be carpeted and the walkways tiled. This should give not only a contrast in texture, but also colour. Another example might be a large outpatients department in a hospital with several reception desks. A different colour scheme could be used for each area.

In this poorly designed reception area, the entrance doors open on different sides, the table is an obstruction, the reception desk is not easily accessible and there are no tactile warnings before the stairs or the lift and no handrail up the stairs.

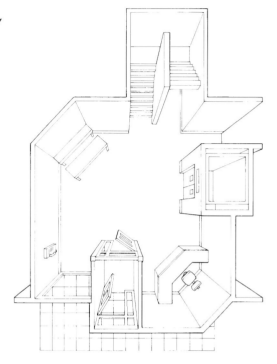

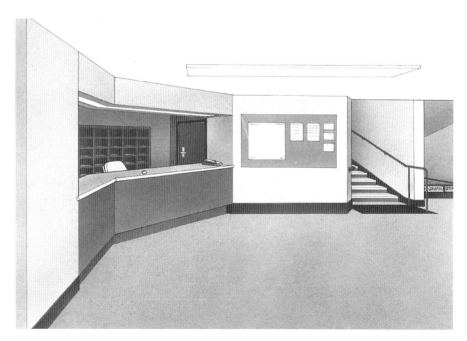

Well designed reception desk with strong tonal contrasts, diffused overhead lighting and strategically placed notice board. The stairs are logically planned and the treads well marked.

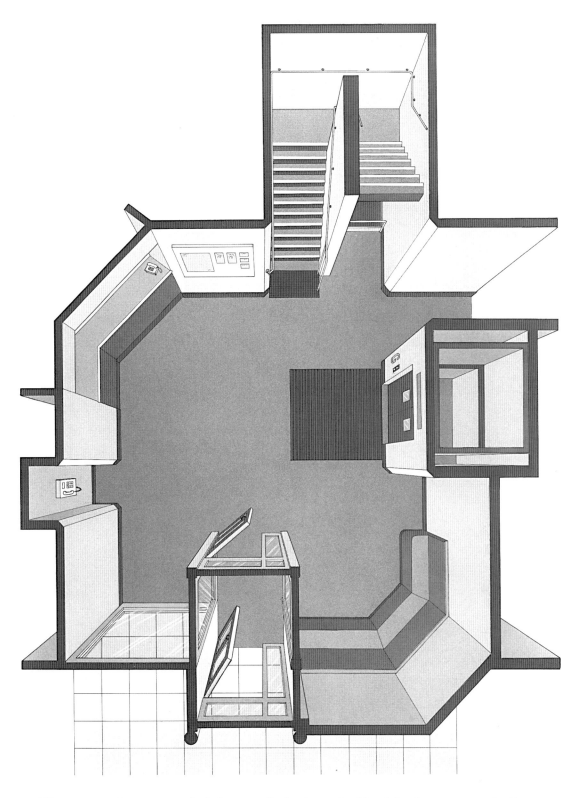

The same plan as top left but well designed. Double doors open in the same direction, the reception desk can be seen from the entrance, the reception furniture does not present a hazard, there are tactile markings in front of the stairs and lift and the telephone is recessed.

Different types of furniture can identify different usages within an overall area: easy chairs for waiting areas, upright chairs and desks for interview areas, and so on.

In a hotel lounge, small light clusters can be used above service areas, with larger lighting units positioned to indicate the direction of travel for walkways through the area. However it is important that a uniform level of illumination is maintained throughout.

Furnishing should be selected so that it contrasts with the floor and the walls. Below knee-height items such as coffee tables are not a good idea in public areas. However in personal environments they may become useful to the occupier who will quickly learn their position. Even then it is important that such items should provide contrast with the floor in both colour and tone.

The general rules of interior decoration, discussed in more detail in Chapter 9, should be adhered to wherever possible.

Restaurants and canteens
Entrance and exit doors should be clearly indicated and fitted with self-closing devices, as described in the internal doors section. The general layout of tables and chairs should be in a regular pattern, not random, with sufficient gangway space to allow easy passage by those in a wheelchair and those with a guide dog: a width of 1.2m is recommended.

Tables and chairs should be colour and tone contrasted with the floor. The general level of lighting should be even and adequate: pools of light and dark should be avoided.

If self-service facilities are available, menus and price lists should be provided in large print and braille. Any wall displays should be properly illuminated. Trays and crockery should be in colours which clearly contrast with each other and with the surface of the tables.

Kitchens and kitchenettes
There are a number of general points to observe in designing these facilities:

- there should be a provision of natural daylight;

- open plan areas and large work surfaces make food preparation more efficient;

- orientation is improved if circulation areas are kept clear of tables and chairs;

- floors must be of a non-slip variety when wet or dry;

- a light, plain-coloured floor, rather than a patterned one, will make dropped items easier to find.

Storage: As with any kitchen, the more storage space the better. It is worth remembering that visually impaired people generally put utensils and stores in the same place each time that they are used. This makes them easier to find and introduces an orderly system to the area. Doors to storage cupboards should be a sliding type: side hung doors can be left open with the attendant risk of collision.

Work top surfaces: These should be non-reflective to avoid visual confusion. It is useful to provide both light and dark coloured working surfaces so that the preparation of different foodstuffs can be done on the appropriate background surface for the best visual contrast. If a single

This kitchen uses maximum contrast to aid visibility. Note the use of dark and light food preparation surfaces, and the strongly contrasting handles and knobs. Plugs are positioned above the work surface, there is a wall-mounted vertical telephone and sliding doors to the cabinets. To avoid glare, eye-level lights are shielded.

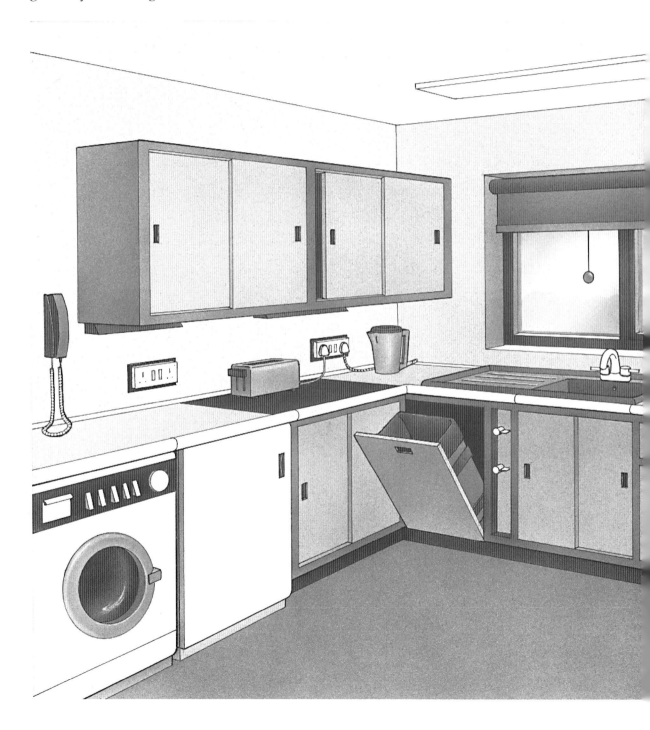

Compact layout for small kitchenette which
includes purpose-built oven, hob and sink unit.

Cupboard handles and sockets
need to be contrasted with their
backgrounds for maximum
visibility.

84

colour work surface is all that can be provided, it should be of a neutral colour, such as grey, against which both light and dark coloured objects will be distinguishable.

A slightly raised edge of hardwood or similar material placed along the leading edge of the worktop will help to contain spills while a cove at the rear of the worktop will seal the joint and assist cleaning.

Lighting: Work surfaces need careful illumination as people with poor sight may have to work in close proximity to them to see what they are doing. This may mean that they end up working in their own shadow, particularly if a single overhead fitting is used in a small kitchen. Additional task lighting should therefore be situated around each area of activity. Fluorescent light gives less shadow, uses less electricity and the tubes last longer than ordinary tungsten lamps.

Work surface or task lighting is best provided by fixing strip lighting to the underneath of wall cupboards or shelves above the work surface. Glass shelves should be avoided.

Unprotected fluorescent fittings may well act as a source of glare so they should be shielded. This shield need only take the form of a piece of material fixed vertically underneath the cupboard alongside the light fitting. However it is important that the depth of this material is calculated to cut off the light at the edge of the work surface, preventing stray light from reaching the floor.

If a kitchen is to be used by many visually impaired people, the level of illumination should be adjustable to suit different eye conditions: someone with light sensitive eyes will require dim lighting whilst someone else may need much higher levels. Even people who are not visually impaired find that their lighting requirements vary from day to day.

Layout: A continuous sequence of units is recommended: work top, sink and cooker. The proximity of the sink to the hob is very important, as the transfer of heavy pans and hot liquids back and forth from hob to sink should be as easy as possible.

The hob should be designed and positioned in such a way that there is a free working surface on both sides wherever possible. Control knobs should be on the front of the hob, preferably on a horizontal rather than vertical plane, so that it is easier to read any tactile markings or see any visual indicators. It should be simple to relate the controls to their various functions.

Various settings of the control knobs should be easy to feel and clearly marked in relief. High marking material and specially made knobs may assist here - these are available from RNIB (see Appendix b: Useful Information).

The oven light needs to be assessed as a potential source of glare. It is useful for the oven to have a sound signal which comes on when the oven is lit, better still if it also has one to indicate whether the oven has reached its correct temperature.

Some manufacturers are now producing appliances which incorporate many of these features. Zanussi has recently produced a washing machine with a user-friendly control

Matt bathroom tiles and diffused light in
this bathroom minimise glare off
reflective surfaces.

Good contrast assists
visibility.

The ideal bathroom uses colour and tone contrast to the maximum. Note contrast between floor and walls, towels and walls, window and blind, shower curtains and bath. Smaller fittings are highlighted by contrast tiles.

panel. This is easier not only for people with a visual impairment, but for everyone.

The location of power points and switches should comply with the Institute of Electrical Engineers Code of Practice. This is critical in the vicinity of the sink, washing machines and similar items where water is being used.

Cooker hoods which extract steam and smells should include lighting which shines down on the hob, but which protect the viewer's eyes from dazzle.

Plugs, sockets and switches: Plugs and sockets should be installed with colour and tone contrast in mind. Plugs with handles are easier for people with poor grip. At least four double sockets should be provided around work tops. This provides for appliances to be located in sensible and safe positions. Mains switches, stopcocks and isolation valves should be easy to reach and identify, with 'on' and 'off' positions clearly marked with high visibility lettering and tactile embossed symbols. All older types of fuse box that involve threading fuse wire through fuse holders should be replaced by modern circuit breaker types which are much easier to reset. It is also worth considering installing a telephone socket in the kitchen.

Bathrooms and toilets
Bathroom walls should be waterproof with an easy to clean surface. The finish should be matt - this is particularly important with finishes such as tiles which can produce high levels of reflection and glare. Matt surface tiles create a much warmer environment in bathrooms and toilets.

The floor should be non-slip, easy to clean, and waterproof. Where carpet is used, it should be rubber-backed. Bathroom fittings such as bath, basin, WC pan and bidets should have a colour or tone that contrasts with the wall and floor finishes.

Items such as hand basins, toilets, toilet roll holders, soap dishes and switches can be highlighted by tiling around them in a contrasting colour. Emergency cords should be easily distinguishable from light pull cords and should be fitted with two knobs, one at normal height, and one just above the floor so that it can be reached from a low level.

Siting of emergency cords is also very important. They should never be placed in inaccessible corners or areas. A fairly thick cord will also aid visibility and be easier to find and grip. In order to differentiate between light pull cords and emergency pull cords different shaped knobs could be used to avoid confusion.

Towel rails, rings and handrails should be securely fixed to the walls and positioned so they can assist elderly or infirm people using the bathroom. Again they should differ in colour and tone with the surface to which they are fixed.

The siting of a mirror over a washbasin requires careful consideration - people may need to get very close, so the positioning should allow this. Light fittings should illuminate the user's face without being visible in the mirror. For this reason, most units which have a light as an integral part of the mirror are unsatisfactory.

Coat hooks at head height in a bathroom or toilet are always a potential hazard, and not just to visually impaired people. Careful siting will help.

Rounded furniture prevents accidents; contrasts between floor, wall and seats aids mobility.

Careful arrangement of dining tables in rows, with at least 1m gap between them, assists people with visual impairment to find their way around. Random, close arrangement is difficult to manoeuvre.

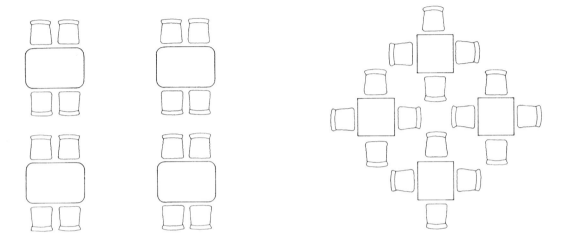

A potentially good dining room but the attempt to maximise natural light has created a glare problem on the polished surfaces; rounded corners on the furniture would have been safer.

Showers

Where showers are fitted, they should be thermostatically controlled. The positioning of a protected light source above the shower cubicle or area is advantageous. Shower heads should contrast with the background - a white shower head against white tiles is a dangerous projection. Where a separate shower cannot be fitted and it has to be integral with the bath, the shower head should be adjustable in height within a range of 1.5m to 2m above floor level. It may be helpful to provide a flexible hose of sufficient length to enable the shower head to be used at the washbasin.

Shower controls should have clearly visible signs, preferably with tactile embossed symbols for on/off and hot/cold.

Bedrooms

Many people with a visual impairment suffer from additional health problems. Whilst this may not necessarily mean long confinements in bed, for design purposes it is worth treating the bedroom as a room to be used throughout the day.

Privacy should be taken into account, particularly when positioning the bed in relation to windows. A bed-ridden person's access to light switches, task lighting, sockets for TV, radios, clock and entry phone should also be considered.

Doors should normally be able to open wide against walls. Many people want to use radios, TV, hi-fi systems, and computers in bedrooms, so there should be adequate provision for related storage.

Despite imposing a degree of rigidity upon the room layout, built-in furniture makes it easier to site power points and controls, and avoids trailing cables. Again, built-in cupboards and wardrobes should be fitted with sliding doors wherever possible and all furniture should have rounded edges and corners to minimise the risk of accidental injury. Consider an internal light inside wardrobes.

Door handles and drawer knobs must be easy to see and should be colour contrasted with the background. They should also comply with the principles laid down in the relevant advisory publications (see Bibliography).

The use of patterned materials for carpets and bedspreads should be avoided as they create visual confusion and make it difficult for dropped articles to be seen. Plain or mottled materials are preferable.

94

Summary of key interior dimensions

The following table sets out key dimensions to be followed in building design:

Blind person using cane	width 750mm
Blind person plus guide dog	width 1.1m length 1.5m
Blind person plus sighted escort	width 1.2m
Blind person with crutches	width 900mm
Doorways	clear opening width 800mm
Corridors	clear width 1.2m
Stairs:	
Riser	150mm
Going or tread	280mm
Edging strip	50mm wide/full width step
Nosing	50-65mm on tread and riser across full width of step
Handrails:	
Height	900mm above pitch line to centre line of handrail
Diameter	45-50mm
Length	300mm horizontal beyond top and bottom step
Tapping rail	100mm minimum 200mm maximum above ground level
Edging or upstart	150mm minimum with handrail. 100mm if no handrail
Eyelevel	1.4 - 1.6m above ground level
Visibility panel/ for highlighting	150mm square or similar surface area
Door handle	Height 1m
Light switch	Height 1.3m

Power socket	Height 350-500mm
Overhead clearance	2.1m minimum 2.5m optimum
Reach from sitting position	1.3m distance height 400mm sideways 250mm backwards
Stairs	Maximum rise between landings 1.2m

Passage widths for different people

750 mm

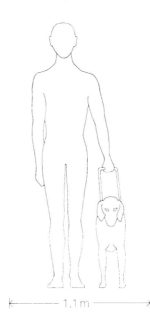

1.1m

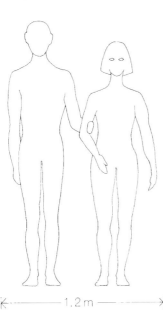

1.2 m

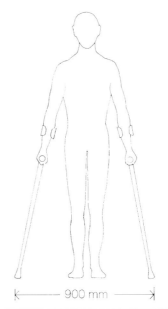

900 mm

Mobility handicap dimensions

The dimensions shown below should include almost all people with mobility handicaps. However, there is much more variation among disabled people than among able-bodied people, so inevitably these dimensions may not accommodate a few special cases.

The following basic data show actual lengths or widths of people plus equipment, and clearance lengths and clear outdoor passage widths needed for those same people plus equipment.

Lengths	Pram plus pusher	900mm
	95th percentile wheelchair	1.14m
	Wheelchair plus pusher	1.75m
	Space for wheelchair	1.25m
	Adult plus guide dog	1.5m
	Powered scooter	1.27m
	Electric pavement vehicle	1.4m (average)
	Double pushchair	1m
Widths	Wheelchair (with elbows)	900mm
	95th percentile wheelchair	670mm (ex. elbows)
	Electric pavement vehicle scooter	800mm
Minimum passage widths*	Stick user	750mm
	Double crutch user	900mm
	Adult and child	1.1m
	Adult plus helper	1.2m
	Adult / guide dog	1.1m

* Minimum passage width includes doorways.
Double doors might need to be split to the proportion 2/3 :1/3 to provide a clear passage.

Lighting

The key issues

Lighting is one of the most important and complex elements of architectural design. Light is the single most important influence in revealing buildings and interiors to their users.

The human visual system depends on light to operate, and appropriate lighting is the most important aid to vision. In simple terms - no light, no sight.

As people get older, their lighting requirement increases: a 60 year old will need considerably more light than a 20 year old. Visually impaired people generally require up to double the quantity of light needed by sighted people, although in some cases such increases may lead to glare problems.

Visual confusion is caused by reflection and glare from shiny surfaces which should therefore be kept to an absolute minimum or avoided altogether.

Care should be taken to ensure that shadows caused by natural or artificial light do not give rise to optical illusions. For example, a shadow could mask, conceal or camouflage a potential obstruction or give the illusion of being the edge of a piece of furniture or part of the building structure. It follows that the means of controlling both artificial and natural light should be provided where possible.

Recommended Chartered Institution of Building Services

98

Engineers (CIBSE) lighting standards are set out later in this chapter.

General lighting

Uniformity of illumination is of great importance when designing the lighting for a new or refurbished building. Many visually impaired people will find it difficult to cope with extreme variations of light. If CIBSE guidelines are followed, variation should be minimised.

What can give rise to problems, however, are variations in brightness that can occur between a luminaire and its background. If a bright light is in the general line of sight, it will tend to determine the adaptation level of the viewer. As a result, looking away to the floor, for example, will make that surface appear darker than it otherwise would. Balance is restored only when the adaptation level is reset. The lesson is to avoid glare by ensuring that all luminaires have an acceptable brightness at normal viewing angles.

It is not the purpose of this book to specify actual luminaires for given areas as the range of available light fitting equipment is vast. However, it would be sensible, before making a final choice, to see the luminaire lit and mounted at the proposed height so that it can be viewed from all likely angles.

The contrast between the luminaire and its background - normally the ceiling - should be comfortable and there should be no hotspots that might prove distracting. The surface beneath should be evenly lit, with no striations or discernible patterns of light.

Fall-off at the edges of the illuminated area should be gradual rather than sharply defined. If the width of the illuminated area - or alternatively the point where the lighting level falls to half that directly beneath the luminaire - can be measured, this gives some guidance to the spacing of the luminaires in a real environment.

Clearly lighting can do much more than just enable something to be seen. It can help to establish where you are in a building, particularly in conjunction with decoration.

A long corridor can be tackled with greater confidence if the far wall is differentiated by light or colour. Illuminated notice boards can mark a boundary; a white push plate on a dark coloured door can show which side opens; a light coloured door in a light coloured wall can be found if surrounded by a dark coloured architrave; a spotlit clock on a wall can aid orientation; switches and sockets can be easily found when they are highlighted by contrasting colours.

There are numerous other examples of where colour, contrast and lighting can work in harness to make environments more easily legible.

On the downside, strong shadows are potentially misleading and can be dangerous. Railway platform lighting with a sharp cut-off can cause visually impaired travellers to 'see' an illusory gap between platform and train. Shadows that make spaces seem longer than they are can cause visually impaired people to walk into walls. The moral is that extreme brightness differences must be avoided: they are more likely to confuse than enlighten.

Bright natural light causes shadows and glare in this entrance hall (below). Overhead lighting causes areas of glare on the ceiling and floor (right).

Poorly designed fittings cause glare on this VDU screen (left); use of louvres, with fittings, controls light and solves the problem (right).

Well designed louvres on light fittings in this store minimise the reflection on the well-defined shop walkway*.

There is no point in having expensive light fittings if they are not accompanied by adequate contrast. In this workroom, the lighting is complemented by reversible work tops for task work, so that small objects may be seen against contrasting backgrounds.

* Courtesy Marks & Spencer.

102

The requirement to ensure adequate lighting levels in all areas is not only a legal obligation on building owners and managers but is also a basic consideration in making a building suitable for its users' needs. Appropriate lighting not only makes things more visible to people with poor sight - it also makes the environment a much safer place for everyone.

Current UK legislation puts responsibility on employers to provide conditions that do not adversely affect the health and safety of their staff. This means that codes of practice are the only authoritative guides.

Guidance documents have been produced by the Department for Education for schools and by the Department of Health for hospitals and health-care buildings. But the main codes of practice for interior lighting are those produced by the Illuminating Engineering Society (IES) and, more recently, the Chartered Institution of Building Services Engineers (CIBSE). However these deal only with the needs of normally sighted people and make few recommendations for those with poor sight.

There is at present no definitive work which makes comprehensive lighting recommendations for visually impaired people. Indeed, their needs vary so widely that it would be difficult to do so. With this in mind, it is perhaps better to take the recommendations for normally sighted people as a starting point and modify these in the light of the anticipated needs of those who are visually impaired. This will often mean providing significantly more light - around twice for general circulation purposes - but much more for specific tasks for those who will benefit. At the same time, the option to dim high levels should be retained for the benefit of those who would find it a handicap.

From our experience of measuring light levels in various buildings, it is apparent that even the basic CIBSE recommendations are seldom implemented, let alone any additional lighting to meet the needs of visually impaired people.

The many issues of lighting therefore demand special attention in all new and refurbished building design projects.

Lighting a corridor

Let us take a corridor as an example. The worst way to light it would be by using bare fluorescent lamps installed in fittings mounted widthways. This would cause maximum discomfort.

To ensure the corridor is well lit and the light is evenly distributed, ceiling mounted fittings should be positioned longitudinally, preferably down the centre line of the corridor, and lamps should be fitted with well designed diffusers or louvres to reduce glare.

Now the walls and floor will be relatively evenly lit and such an arrangement should be acceptable, if not ideal, to anyone who finds high lighting levels a problem.

Lighting a stairway

Another common lighting problem is posed by stairways. Here lighting and decor must go hand in hand. The stair covering should not have a pattern that can cause confusion between tread and riser or between one tread and another.

104

These photographs and diagrams from the CIBSE Code of Practice for Interior Lighting* demonstrate three types of lighting:

General lighting system
This employs a regular array of luminaires to provide a uniform illuminance across the working plane.

Indirect lighting system
This uses luminaires located adjacent to the work stations to provide indirect illuminance. The necessary illumination in the surrounding areas is provided by additional luminaires as required.

Task lighting system
This employs luminaires, located at the work station, to provide the necessary task illuminance. A general lighting scheme is used to provide the ambient illuminance for the main area.

* Courtesy of CIBSE Code 1984

General lighting system (top).
Indirect lighting system (middle).
Work station or task lighting (bottom).

106

A contrasting colour of nosing can help but this must not be so wide that one step merges into the next when viewed from above.

Changes in direction should be clearly visible, particularly if this involves a change in tread depth which destroys the climbing rhythm.

Lighting on stairs should be sufficient to highlight any obstructions on the flight of stairs, but should highlight the treads as opposed to the risers to emphasize each step.

It is very important that ceiling-mounted luminaires do not become a glare source - they should be well shielded. Alternatively, large-area, low-brightness sources can be mounted on a side or facing wall. This has the added advantage of easy maintenance.

A fashion for incorporating lighting into handrails is universally disliked by visually impaired people. The rail usually becomes a glare source at some point in their field of vision.

Spotlighting

An area lit only by narrow beam spotlights can create unacceptable contrasts and cause problems of adaptation. However, using spotlights to supplement the general illumination over a small task area can be very effective, providing that the general illumination is adequate for normal purposes. For instance, in an office lit to around 500 lux, using an adjustable reading lamp to raise the task area to 1,000 lux or 1,500 lux can be quite acceptable. Using the same reading lamp in an area lit to 50 lux will probably cause problems.

At the other extreme, flat illumination can give rise to problems due to the lack of visual clues, but this is best solved by careful choice of decoration.

Uplighting

The advantages of free-standing uplights is that they can be positioned to suit activities. The inherent inefficiency of bouncing light off the ceiling is offset by the use of very efficient types of lamp.

Reflections off a lit office ceiling in the screen of a VDU are certainly less distracting than those of ceiling-mounted luminaires. However, if the space between ceiling and uplighter is less than 1.5m a visually impaired person can find an uplit ceiling unacceptably bright, resulting in discomfort. An acceptable compromise may be found by combining an uplighter installation with local task lighting, balancing adequate general illumination with localised brighter light for work.

Lighting controls

Tungsten: With ordinary tungsten filament lamps, dimming is simple. There is a wide range of dimmer units that can be substituted for ordinary light switches. Some have a rotary knob to switch on and adjust the light level while others have a similar system with the addition of a press on/off action to retain the rotary setting.

There is also a version which requires only a touch to turn on or off. If the touch is maintained, it will cycle through its range of dimming. This is particularly useful for those who find it difficult to grasp things and the touch may be with the back of the hand or even the nose.

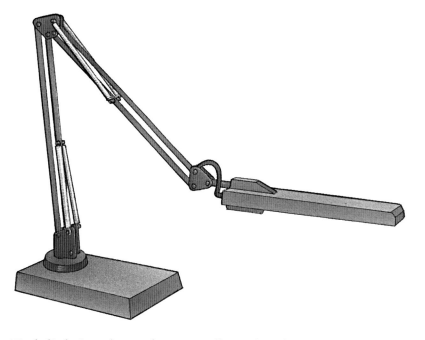

Task lighting: lamp for partially sighted people has a hood to shield the user from glare. The compact fluorescent lamp has a low surface temperature and so is especially suitable for close reading work.

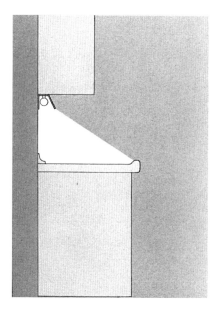

Task lighting under a kitchen cupboard; the reflector prevents glare at eye level.

Good overhead use of daylight
and high level fittings cause
minimum glare in this corridor.

Natural overhead light enhances the contrasting finishes
and colours; rounded furniture and well defined doors
make this an easy and safe reception to negotiate.

110

It is worth remembering that in accommodation for older people, the population is likely to change from time to time and being able to change the lighting level is of considerable importance. A dimmer is a much cheaper solution than attempting to change lamps or luminaires.

Fluorescent: With fluorescent lamps, dimming is not so simple. With the new low energy light bulbs or compact fluorescent lamps (CFLs), dimming is not always possible. CFLs are a useful and economic replacement for tungsten filament lamps in domestic situations.

In heavy usage situations, dimmable fluorescent units are more viable and many installations now incorporate this feature as an aid to energy saving. Using an electronic ballast which operates the lamp at a very high frequency, flicker is avoided and efficiency improved. Although dimmable high frequency fluorescent units are more expensive than a conventional system, the additional cost can usually be recovered in energy savings and more flexible lighting levels.

High frequency fluorescent lamps minimise the problem of flicker, particularly assisting people relying on peripheral vision where flicker is most likely to be detected.

Step changes
While a continuously variable system will enable lighting preferences to be met exactly, step changes can be installed at a much lower price. For instance, a four lamp fluorescent luminaire could be wired so that two lamps could be switched at a time, enabling the illumination to be doubled or halved, on demand. Taken a stage further, three switches would give a choice of one, two, three or four lamps. This

system can also be applied to luminaires in a row, but here the disadvantage may be the unevenness that could result from switching off individual luminaires.

Task lighting

A visually impaired person may require high levels of illumination which are best achieved by placing the light source close to the task. At the same time he or she may also need to work in close proximity to the task so that head, task and luminaire are extremely close together. When a filament lamp is used this can result in what has become known as the 'burnt ear syndrome.'

Fortunately the filament lamp can usually be replaced by a modern compact fluorescent version that provides the same amount of light using between a third and a quarter of the power. Because of the way the gas discharge lamp operates, the surface temperature remains low. A good example is the 11W adjustable reading lamp available from the Partially Sighted Society, high street electrical retailers, and larger DIY stores.

Not all task lighting solutions are achieved with adjustable reading lamps. In some situations - for example, hotel reception desks - it is usually done by spotlights mounted directly above the task. Again, this method has disadvantages for those who need to be close to the task, where they would cast a strong shadow. In such cases an adjustable reading lamp at the reception desk would do much to alleviate the problem.

Daylighting

While daylight is the standard by which all other light sources are judged, it has both advantages and disadvantages. Even an overcast day can provide far more

112

light than will be found in any artificial situation; and bright sunlight is measured in tens of thousands of lux. However the rapid changes caused by passing clouds can bring problems of adaptation.

Indoors, daylight is usually the greatest source of glare. Elaborate methods are often adopted to reduce its effect; these can be films applied to the window glass to reduce visible and solar radiation, or tinted glazing and structural shielding methods. In the absence of these solutions, people resort to vertical or horizontal louvre blinds which bring problems of adjustment and maintenance.

Daylight supplements artificial electric light and of course advantage should be taken of this free light source. Even so, proper provision must be made to control daylight when it becomes more of a hindrance than a help.

On the following page, the CIBSE Code recommendations for task illuminance are set out. Observance of the recommendations of the Code is usually 'deemed to satisfy' any legal requirements for the provision of lighting.

CIBSE recommendations on task illuminance:

Location		Maintained illuminance* (lux)
Entrances	halls, lobbies, waiting rooms	200
Enquiry desks		500
Circulation	corridors, lifts, stairs	100
Lounges	communal	100-300
Kitchens	food preparation	150-300
Bedrooms		100
Offices	general	500
Computer work stations		300-500
Filing rooms		300

Evaluating lighting proposals

This chapter has dealt with some of the key issues in the provision of better lighting to meet the needs of visually impaired people. The following checklist may assist when appraising lighting proposals:

- Glare should be avoided at all costs. Check the brightness of luminaires at all normal viewing angles and look for surfaces which might give glaring reflections.

- Areas should be lit to the levels recommended in the CIBSE Code with additional allowance made to cater for the needs

* Maintained illuminance is the average value obtained immediately before maintenance is carried out, ie before the luminaire is cleaned and the lamp cleaned or replaced.

114

of visually impaired people. Generally the additional allowance should be 25 per cent to 50 per cent above the CIBSE recommendation.

- Light should be evenly distributed with no dramatic changes when moving from one area to another, for example from a work area to a corridor.

- Task lighting should be an essential part of the lighting system for people with a visual impairment, as well as an aid to everyone else. It is an economic way of raising the task illuminance without substantial increases in energy consumption.

- Where appropriate, the lighting level should be controlled by dimming or switching so that the illuminance can be adjusted to meet individual needs. This becomes especially important in residential accommodation.

Chapter 7

Interior decoration

The way in which interior spaces are decorated and finished can make an enormous contribution to quality of life for people with a visual handicap. A lot of the key themes - such as the need to create environments which are visually uncluttered and uncomplicated through the use of colours and contrast, and to avoid optically difficult patterns for wall and floor finishes - have already been introduced earlier in this book.

The basic principles of interior decoration can be summarised as follows:

- Walls should be finished in pale tones with all surfaces being matt.

- Floorings should be plain without optically confusing patterns, and not gloss finished to produce glare or dazzle. The floor finish should contrast with the walls.

- Ceilings should be finished in pale colours to help reflect available light more evenly throughout the area.

- Doors should contrast with the surrounding walls so they can be easily identified. Door furniture should also contrast with the door.

- Items such as sockets, switches, pull cords, handles and so on, should be contrasted with their background so that they can be easily located.

116

• Soft furnishings should contrast with both walls and floors. The introduction of simple patterns in a room should be carefully considered: greater variety should be balanced against the potential for visual confusion, for example in locating keys or coins on a highly patterned bedspread.

This chapter develops some of the basic considerations with regard to interior decoration.

Wall finishes
Walls should be finished in plain, matt colours. A further step to create user-friendly interiors for people with poor sight would be to use generally pale colours for walls and ceilings. This not only maximises the available light, but also helps to distribute it evenly.

An eggshell finish is satisfactory, but a matt finish is preferable where glare may cause problems. Rough finishes such as pebbledash should be avoided because some visually impaired people may wish to trail their hand along the wall in order to locate specific items. Trailing boards can be affixed along brick walls, etc to avoid hurt to trailing hands. Different tactile surfaces on walls can also be used strategically to aid orientation.

There is some scope to use small-patterned wallpapers in given areas. This can be useful to highlight chimney breasts or other features and to help make the area more aesthetically pleasing to people with full sight. For many visually impaired people, a small patterned wallpaper can appear almost plain and therefore will not contribute significantly to environmental clutter and confusion. However wallpapers with bold or large-scale patterns cause general visual confusion and may make objects on shelves difficult to locate. Embossed wallpapers such as anaglypta, when finished with emulsion paint, are perfectly satisfactory, creating an interesting surface which is still user-friendly to people with poor sight.

Skirting boards and dado rails should be in a contrasting colour to provide additional help in navigating an area safely. These can be particularly useful for people left with only a small amount of side vision, offering valuable assistance in maintaining the line of travel along a corridor.

The use of floor-to-ceiling mirrors to create the illusion of space is a source of potential danger to visually impaired people, greatly distorting any realistic perception of space.

Glass, too, can create problems, although here the problem is one of invisibility rather than reflection. Where areas are divided by plain glass screens or glass floor-to-ceiling partitions, the glass must be made visible with horizontal bands or some form of decorative motif at eye level. Patterned glass, though less problematic, should be treated in a similar fashion.

Floor patterns
Highly patterned carpets with a swirl or decorative tiles will create a great deal of visual confusion and could effectively 'hide' small articles inadvertently dropped onto the floor. Patterned floor coverings also alter the perceived shape of objects placed upon them, such as furniture, particularly where the colour of the object is fairly close to the hue of the carpet or floor covering. At worst, such patterns will make a visually impaired person feel apprehensive and uncomfortable in traversing a space.

Two versions of the same interior. The room as seen by
someone with full vision (top).

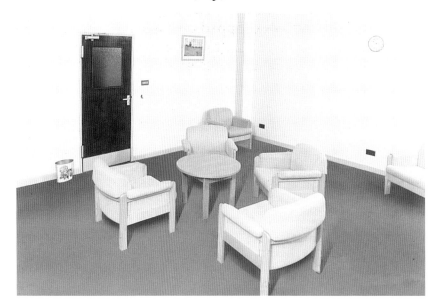

The same room as seen by someone who is visually
impaired (bottom). This room demonstrates the
importance of contrast between walls and floor, doors
and furniture in negotiating a space.

Busy patterns cause confusion. A bunch of keys dropped on a light coloured small scale design (top) is easier to find than on a large, dark design (bottom).

Doors, door furniture and switches should be contrasted with their backgrounds so that they can be easily identified.

Also, they could result in people with poor sight colliding with chairs and settees.

Door details

In terms of decoration, doors should provide a good level of contrast with the walls and the floor where possible. The door should be clearly visible as a vertical rectangle finished in a different tone to the wall in which it is situated. This does not necessarily imply the use of garish colours - a dark grey door against a pale grey wall will provide a sufficient degree of contrast for most people. Remember that a dark red door situated in a dark green wall, whilst providing lively colour contrast, will offer very little in the way of tonal contrast.

Door furniture should also be clearly visible. It can be highly frustrating to someone with poor sight to have to search for a door handle. This problem is easily solved as modern products come in a wide range of finishes and colours.

A problem arises in very old or listed buildings where black wrought-iron door furniture may be mounted on a dark, oak-stained door. It is often not possible to paint the door furniture for historical and aesthetic reasons. A simple solution is to insert a small plastic sheet of a contrasting colour behind the door handle, using the existing door furniture fixtures to secure it. No permanent modifications have been made and the door is easily restored to its original appearance.

It is also useful to highlight the edges of doors, windows and so on in order to minimise the risk of collision if they are inadvertently left in a half-open position.

All doors should have spring closures or be hung on rising butt hinges to prevent them being left half open. Side doors and windows should not open into a corridor where a visually impaired person might collide with them. Bomber hinges should not be used.

Where doors are numbered, the digits should contrast with the door surface in colour and/or tone, and be raised at least 2mm. Door numbers should be around 60mm in height and fitted at or just above average eye level (1.525m).

Signs mounted on doors should be designed in accordance with recommended practice: pale lower case letters on a matt dark coloured background. Again, these should be situated at around eye level. A sign in braille may also be an appropriate option.

The option of highlighting a door simply by painting its frame and the architrave in contrasting colour has its merits. However its use must be carefully considered, especially where a door closes across the corridor and may be visually misinterpreted.

Soft furnishings
Although bold patterns should generally be avoided to minimise visual confusion, there is no doubt that under certain circumstances they can make objects more visible.

One example might be a settee with a highly patterned fabric covering in a room with a carpet of plain or mottled style. In this instance, the settee will be highly visible, particularly if its background colour is tonally different from that of the carpet. (Even so a visually impaired person will still have difficulty in recovering items lost from the pocket when seated on the settee. That is why fabrics of a relatively plain or mottled style are generally preferred.)

Another positive use of patterns would be where they are deployed to give a focal point to an otherwise plain area - curtains, for example. As always, context is everything.

Chapter 8
Signs and notices

Key principles

Even in the best-planned environment, there will be a need for signs and notices. These basic principles should be adhered to when catering for the needs of people with a visual impairment:

- signs need to be simple, short and easily understood

- location of signs should be part of the process of planning the building and environment

- signs should be consistent, using prescribed typefaces, colours and other graphic devices

- signs and notices must inspire confidence through clarity.

For visually impaired people, the first problem is to locate the sign. Signs should be placed in a logical position and be obviously identifiable. The sign board must contrast with the background against which it is seen and the lettering should contrast with the sign board. In the case of corporate signage where the sign board colour cannot be changed, a contrasting border should be put around the sign. The border width should be 10 per cent of the width of the sign.

The position of signs needs to be considered in the context of the overall design so that they do not constitute an obstruction and so that adequate illuminination can be provided at all times. Signs are difficult to identify and read

124

if they are positioned against a background of low level sunlight or artificial light.

Legibility

There is much debate within the blind community about contrast and strength value of various colours. Research into these issues has been commissioned by RNIB.

On the best evidence we have, the following points suggest the most effective options:

- the legibility of signs is improved for people with a visual impairment if, in general, white lettering is set on a dark background;

- lower case (non-capitalised) lettering is generally easier to read;

- fixing the sign at eye level (between 1.4 and 1.6m above floor level) with easy access for close-up viewing is an advantage for all;

- to minimise glare, avoid reflective glass cases and ensure that the sign has a matt surface.

The following chart gives guidance on the colour contrast which should be used against some of the most commonly used backgrounds for signs, such as brick, stone, whitewashed walls or green vegetation.

Schedule of colour contrast

Background	Sign board	Legend
Red brick or dark stone	White	Black, dark green or dark blue
Light brick or light stone	Black/dark	White/yellow
Whitewashed wall	Black/dark	White/yellow
Green vegetation	White	Black, dark green or dark blue

Tactile signs

Tactile signs are essential for people with no sight at all or those whose vision is only sufficient to locate a sign but not distinguish individual characters.

A tactile sign must be positioned where it can be easily touched, that means at a height of between 1.4m and 1.7m and at a forward distance of approximately half a metre. To be effective, a tactile sign must be embossed, not engraved. RNIB can provide information about manufacturers of tactile signs.

The depth of embossing must be 1mm to 1.5mm and the stroke width 1.5mm to 2mm. The edges should be slightly rounded - a half-round section is not acceptable. The minimum character height should be 15mm, the maximum 60mm. Some thought needs to be given on usage, for example, a tactile sign above each coat hook can be a useful clue to the location of coats in cloakrooms, etc.

Visual and tactile toilet sign with maximum contrast.

Ideally, door signs should communicate clearly through visual, tactile and braille using upper and lower case letters.

Sign boards can be dangerous obstructions on the pavement.

Clearly signed exit door at waist level.

Visual and tactile sign above lift call button.

The pictures on the left and in the centre show signs* using a pictogram-based system for visually impaired people and students with learning difficulties; the picture on the right is a detail of the tactile sign board used to locate braille messages.

* Courtesy Henshaw's Society for the Blind; signs by brand id.

128

A tactile version of Helvetica bold sans serif is acceptable, giving an opportunity to combine a visible and tactile sign.

Braille
Where space and cost permit, braille may also be used. For single word signs, it is permissible to use grade 1 braille. For multi-word signs, contracted braille must be used.

Some thought needs to be given to the positioning of braille signs. If they are low, the braille message will initially be 'upside down' to the reader's fingers, requiring the reader to crouch. Some braille signs are located on a 'braille bar' 1m above the floor, enabling the user to stand and read.

With a tactile sign meant to be located by touch, it must be easy to locate by touch and well positioned, preferably allowing the reader to get close to it.

High visibility and tactile signs should always be used on or adjacent to:

- toilet doors
- bathroom doors
- bedroom doors
- lift call buttons
- the top and bottom of flights of stairs
- wherever else it is necessary to show the function of a room.

Talking signs
These are now a possibility, triggered by remote control, and can be cheaply and easily installed. Wording must be informative and effective.

Symbols or pictograms

Where symbols or pictograms are used, they should be of a standard design, if one is available, or as simple and uncomplicated as possible if not. They should comply with the general provisions of signs in terms of colour contrasting, size, use of tactile embossed systems where appropriate, and so on.

Reading signs and notices

Loss of peripheral vision on one side, caused by damage to the optic pathways between the back of the eye and the visual cortex, has particular implications for reading signs and notices. If the loss is to the left, at the end of a written line, the difficulty will be getting back to the beginning of the next line. In most cases the eye will stop far short of the beginning of the line and recommence reading some way along it. The sentence will, of course, not make any sense so the person will then spend time scanning around the page in order to locate where they have made the error.

To help with this particular instance, a bright coloured band down the left-hand side of a notice or a page may be helpful. This would help the person to locate the beginning of a line, making notices easier to read.

A further problem when scanning from the end of one line to the beginning of the next is that many people inadvertently slip two or three lines and therefore begin reading at a different place to the correct one. Sometimes this slippage is upwards to a previously read line, or downwards to a line which they have not yet come to. In some instances, the same line is read twice.

130

If the loss in the visual field is on the right side (right hemi-anopia) most of the above problems will be eliminated. However, a new set of problems present themselves, as the word which is about to be read will be invisible until it pops up in the very central area of vision. Furthermore, the end of the line may not be recognised. The technique of using a coloured band down the right-hand side of the page would therefore be of assistance to people with this particular condition.

Whether the loss is to the right or the left, reading notices and signs is clearly going to be difficult and slow.

Chapter 9
Using other senses

When people move around within the built environment, they continually use a combination of senses to orientate themselves and to negotiate obstacles. When one of the senses is removed, or its effectiveness reduced, there is greater dependence on the others.

Sound

To a blind person, sound is a potentially helpful and positive source of information, but one that may sometimes cause confusion. A familiar auditory clue is the bleeper at a pelican crossing, which helps in two ways: first, it helps the blind pedestrian locate the crossing, and second, it indicates whether or not it is safe to cross.

Similar auditory clues or beacons could be provided in and around buildings to aid orientation and warn of hazards. Sound beacons could be installed at the entrance to a building to indicate to a visually impaired person that they have arrived at their destination. There could also be a spoken message to give the name of the building or occupier and some brief instructions on how to enter the building.

The common sounds within buildings also provide people with clues, and great care should be taken not to suppress or eliminate them totally. Inside a shop, for example, the sound of a cash register will direct the visitor to a place where they are able to get assistance.

132

In a restaurant or café the sound of preparation and serving of food might be helpful.

The rumbling noise from escalators, or the chimes that sound when lift doors open, help direct people to vertical circulation routes in a building. Fountains can aid wayfinding in landscaped surroundings.

Conversely, unnecessary noises which tend to swamp useful audible clues should be avoided. Background music played too loud in shops, public houses and restaurants can obliterate useful noises and result in disorientation and tension.

In office environments, the background noise level should be kept below 65 db, whereas in factory statutes, the upper limit is 85 db. Forthcoming EC legislation is likely to reduce these limits by 5-10 db, and designers will be well advised, therefore, to ensure that ambient noise level is kept to well below the statutory limits.

Those without any sensory disability may well become irritated by some of the auditory clues that help visually impaired people. Not everyone likes to hear a bleeper or a spoken message continually broadcasting outside a building.

Various devices have now been developed which overcome this problem, ensuring that the message is transmitted only when there is a blind person in the immediate vicinity. One of these is RNIB's React System, which consists of two elements: a small transmission card carried by the blind person; and a receiver with an audible message. As the blind person approaches, the receiver is activated and broadcasts the appropriate message. This system has been used successfully in railway stations, theme parks, and so on.

There are other electronic systems available which can be used as a means of calling for assistance or for direction-finding. This is a rapidly developing area that designers might investigate in order to make provision for incorporating such devices into building design in due course.

Because many people with a visual impairment are in the older age range, they may also have some sort of hearing problem. In buildings where older people live or visit frequently, as many wayfinding clues as possible should be provided.

Induction loop systems to help the hard of hearing could be installed. The major cost with such systems is the amplifier, although this could be simply attached to wiring, if the wiring were to be built-in at the outset. Designers should be aware of the various factors that can adversely affect the performance of induction loops or infra-red systems. For example, high gloss floors and wall finishes can cause reflection of infra-red beams and seriously distort sound reproduction. The correct installation of such systems requires specialist knowledge.

People who are deafblind have a combination of impairments which create difficulties that exceed the sum of the individual impairments. Resources to develop their independence are sadly scarce. However there are design features that can assist them. Organisations such as Sense (for younger deafblind people), the National Deafblind League, and RNIB can offer help in this area.

On a very basic level, the technology now exists for deafblind people to be made aware of visitors to their home by front door attention buttons which activate a vibrating ring on the person's finger. Vibrating pads beneath pillows to indicate fire or other emergency and type-talk systems for the telephone are also available.

Aromas

In some ancient cultures it was normal practice to impregnate mortar or similar bonding materials with herbs, which would differentiate one area of a building from another. Some timbers, such as cedars and redwood, give off distinctive fragrances which can also be used as wayfinding aids.

In outdoor areas, fragrant plants can improve the environment for all, and provide pleasure and orientation clues for people with poor sight. Plants produce fragrance from leaves and stems, as well as from flowers, and the tactile qualities of various plants can also be used for landmarking and wayfinding. The environment would benefit from a greater exploration of the properties of various plants as aromatic clue-givers.

One issue to bear in mind is to recognise that many species of plants have a limited season, so planning to provide an aromatic experience throughout the year will be necessary, by combining groupings of plants that can provide a continuity throughout the seasons.

Indoor places like laundries, washrooms, kitchens, coffee areas and so on can all be identified through aroma. It may be impractical to manipulate the position of these activities on a site, but it is important to recognise that the clues they produce will aid orientation as visually impaired people make enhanced use of the sense of smell.

A number of commercial companies now produce machines, operated by battery or electrically from a mains supply that produce pleasant aromas. These have obvious usage in certain areas of buildings, but could also be used as wayfinding clues if some thought is given to different aromas in different locations.

Other sensory input
The movement of air and the temperature of air currents are also important clues as to what is going on in an environment. Kinaesthetic information derived from the faculty which perceives voluntary motions of the body can be as important as sounds and aromas.

One blind person comments on air movements in a corridor: 'It gives you information about length and possibly the height. If you come through a swing door the waft of current from both sides would give you quite a clue to width and lengths.'

Visually impaired people need to move around within the environment to establish detail, so designers should appreciate they will not only receive a variety of sensory information, they will actively seek it out in a process called 'mental mapping.'

Mental mapping is described by a blind person: 'It's the use of everything you could possibly use... I store them up in a sort of pigeonhole mind. I know on every tube station I have ever been to which way to go out, from the change points to where to go to the gents. I do it by whether it's

136

down a slope, or down three steps... To the left or right, or something static like a telephone kiosk.'

Sterile environments devoid of sounds, smells and other sensory input are duller for everyone, but they make life much more difficult on a practical level for people with a visual impairment.

Chapter 10

Building services

General

The design practicalities set out in previous chapters apply as much to building services as anything else. Equipment controls to which people require access should be logically planned and positioned, colour- and tone-contrasted, adequately illuminated and, where appropriate, include tactile symbols.

Door entry and exit systems

The door entry system, whether using a simple key, card or coded push-button, must be in an easy-to-find, accessible position. This is best achieved by positioning it on the latch side of the door at a height of between 1m and 1.3m above floor level. The system should also be positioned close to the door frame rather than set back.

The lock or key pad should be colour- or tone-contrasted with the background against which it is seen. Depending on the hardware, this may need to be achieved by using a surround, border or backplate.

Door entry systems need to be adequately illuminated.

The operating method of some door entry systems is inherently complicated and user-unfriendly. For example, card systems requiring the card to be inserted from the bottom or at an oblique angle, or where it is not clear which end of the card needs to be inserted first, have been known

138

to make life difficult and stressful for disabled or elderly people. Such systems should be avoided where possible. A better system uses a keyfob which releases the door lock when the fob is in the proximity of the electronic reading mechanism.

In the case of key pad systems, the push-buttons should not be so small that they are difficult to operate by people with limited manual dexterity. The keys should not be so sensitive that they can be pressed in error. A good guide is an operating pressure of 7 Newtons, with a travel distance of approximately 4mm. The numbers should be clear and distinct and if a ten figure keyboard is used the '5' should be highlighted with an embossed mark. Keypads should be laid out to resemble the telephone number layout, as many people with a visual impairment will be familiar with this.

In some cases, it is necessary to have an exit security system which can only be operated from inside the building. The traditional method has been to use a crash bar on fire door exits. However, electronic systems are now more frequently used. If these are operated by a press-button or pad, care should be taken again to ensure that the control is logically positioned, clearly visible, easy to find, and again uses the telephone number keypad layout.

A useful system is to ensure that a large push-pad is used on the door frame and positioned at the end of a dado rail or hand rail.

Lifts
Lift design decisions are usually made by multinational lift manufacturers, not interior designers or architects. However it is our belief that sound advice should find its

way back to decision makers at all levels and in all disciplines. Design professionals are therefore encouraged to advocate such recommendations to manufacturers and suppliers at every opportunity.

Lift cabins: General principles of contrast and tone apply here, but due to the usual lack of visual stimuli in lift cabins, it is advisable to provide additional assistance by using audible and tactile methods of information.

The position of controls inside and outside the lift is important, as they must be accessible to people in wheelchairs, people with restricted height, or small children.

The minimum internal dimensions should be 1.4m deep by 1.1m wide. This is the minimum size to give access to people in wheelchairs or those with a guide dog, sighted escort, pram, trolley, and so on.

The internal lighting should be of a medium level of intensity, approximately 50-75 lux at floor level. The light should be as uniformly distributed as possible and the use of spotlights should be avoided.

The internal walls of the lift cabin should be covered with a non-reflective matt material preferably in a colour which contrasts with the colour of the floor (which should also have a matt finish). Highly reflective, or mirrored walls cause extreme visual confusion. In smaller lifts a mirror at the rear of the lift cabin may be required to assist people in wheelchairs. This mirror should not be the full height of the cabin, but should be mounted between 1.0m and 1.3m above floor level. If the walls are decorated in any way, for example with advertising material, any glass or perspex cover should be non-reflective.

A handrail along both sides and the back wall of a lift can be helpful to people who may need support. This should be positioned at a height of approximately 1m above floor level.

The lift controls should be positioned at a maximum height above floor level of 1.4m. The bottom of the control panel should not be below 900mm. An optimum arrangement might be to have a control panel say, 200mm deep extending from a height of 1.15m to 1.35m. The control panel should be fitted on the left or right hand side wall and at a distance of 400mm minimum from the front wall of the lift. This improves access for people in wheelchairs. Control panels set close to the corner of a lift can be inaccessible.

The control buttons should be colour contrasted and with control buttons backlit and the legend on the button both visible and tactile (embossed, not engraved). It is not necessary to repeat the legend in braille. A satisfactory control button is that made by Dewhurst, model No. US/89, which is approved by RNIB. Many other manufacturers can supply a similar control button.

On any lift covering more than three floors an audible indication of floor level should be used. Even on a lift travelling between only two floors, it is reassuring for a visually impaired person to have an audible announcement of floor level. Modern digitised speech systems are very flexible and the message can easily be changed.

The door opening time should be set to allow unhurried movement in and out of the lift for those with a mobility restriction.

Door closing should be controlled by photocell or proximity switches to prevent them closing against an obstruction. This requirement was introduced into Building Regulations Part M in the revised edition published in 1992.

Touch sensitive strips in the door edges should be regarded only as a secondary safety system.

Location: The lift should be easy to find so the colour of the lift doors should contrast with the wall finish in the vicinity. The lift call button will be more visible if it is mounted on the wall adjacent to the lift rather than in the lift door frame. The call button should be highlighted by the use of colour contrasting.

The floor level should be indicated on the wall adjacent to or just above the call button using both clear letters and a tactile form.

Escalators and travelators
Escalators: Although escalators provide a very convenient method of moving large numbers of people rapidly through a building, they can present a barrier if they are not carefully designed. In any event, there should always be a lift, stairs or ramp as an alternative for people in wheelchairs, those with a guide dog or anyone who, for whatever reason, does not wish to use an escalator.

The entry and exit to the escalator must be clearly visible and well illuminated. There should be a corduroy pattern

142

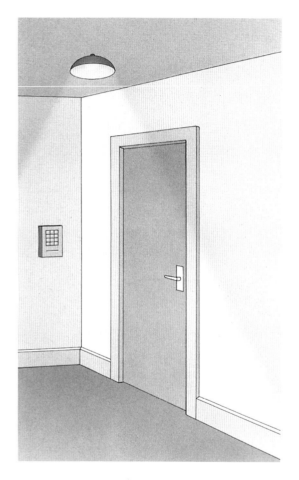 

Two versions of same lobby. Above confusion is caused by the lack of contrast, the shadows cast by the single overhead spotlight, no guide rail and the inaccessibility of the entry call buttons.

In this good version, diffused lighting and maximum contrast help the user to find the entry call buttons, via the handrail, adjacent to the door.

Lift exterior showing well grouped floor number and lift buttons.

Controls inside lifts should be accessible to people in wheelchairs and have large, maximum contrast control buttons.

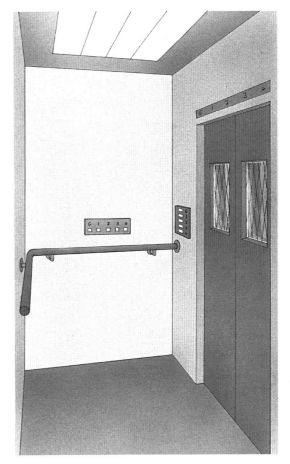

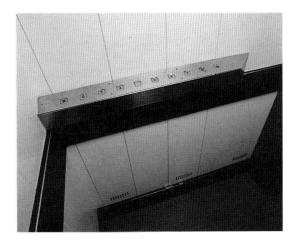

Horizontal lift controls are more accessible for everyone.

144

tactile warning pad, like that used for stairs, at both the entry and exit from the escalator. The direction of movement of the escalator should be indicated by a red or green light.

Most people will enter an escalator on the right-hand side where it would be helpful to indicate with a high visibility and tactile sign whether the escalator is moving up or down. The side panels of the escalator channel should be finished in a non-reflective surface. Back illuminated side panels can be very disorientating . The moving handrail should extend beyond the entry and exit point by at least 150mm. The handrail should be colour and tone contrasted with its surround.

The area at the top and bottom of the escalator should be unrestricted and free from unnecessary obstructions such as portable pedestal-type signboards and display racks. Although background noise is generally to be avoided, some noise from an escalator, particularly in a relatively open environment such as a railway station or shopping mall, provides a very useful clue to its location.

Travelators: Design requirements for travelators are naturally similar to those of escalators. A significant difference is that there is no warning of the imminent end of your journey by steps and handrail flattening out. On a travelator, warning must be given by ensuring that there is good colour and tone contrast between the moving floor of the travelator and the fixed floor immediately at its end. Good lighting in the area should also be provided.

Valves and switches

Isolation valves, switches, fuse panels and so on, should be positioned so that they are easily accessible to people with lack of vision and physical agility. It is unfortunately common practice in housing design to have the water stopcock fitted at a low level in a corner of the kitchen, in all probability inside a fitted cupboard. Similarly the fuse box or reset buttons will be found high up on a wall where access can only be gained by use of steps or a ladder. In an emergency situation, this type of equipment needs to be accessed easily and quickly by any user. So it will benefit everyone, not only visually impaired people, to site them more sensibly.

Heating and air-conditioning controls

The main problem facing visually impaired people in operating such controls is reading the instructions or scales on switches and control knobs. Setting programmers with times or thermostats with temperatures can be particularly problematical.

Many of these problems can be overcome by using equipment that has embossed tactile indicators and high visibility numbers or characters on scales.

This equipment should be positioned where it is accessible, clearly visible and well illuminated. If a control panel is surface mounted, care should be taken to ensure that an unsuspecting person walking close to the wall will not bump into it.

It is important that radiators and hot water pipes are not placed adjacent to the WC or any other area where there is a danger of being burnt. Low surface-temperature radiators are an option but these too must be carefully sited.

146

Emergency call systems

It is often appropriate to have an emergency call system in a toilet, bathroom or kitchen. A continuous cord stretching from ceiling to just above floor level should be used. The cord should be fairly thick - so that it is easy to grip. It may be helpful to provide two knobs, one just above floor level and another attached between 1m and 1.25m above floor level. The cord and knob should be brightly coloured to contrast with the background against which they are seen. Red is a good colour to use as it is traditionally associated with emergency systems.

In a facility that is going to be used by many poorly sighted people, it is a good idea to provide an audible clue to the location of the pull cord such as small bells or rods that ring and chime with minimal touch or movement. These are a constant reminder of the position of the emergency pull cord.

If an emergency button is used, it should be well positioned, clearly visible and have a pressing area large enough to be operated by a person with restricted manual dexterity. The button should feel positive and it should be surrounded by a raised bezel to prevent accidental operation. An operating force of around 7 Newtons with a movement of approximately 4mm is recommended.

For deafblind people, a personal vibrating pager can give indication of a ringing doorbell, a ringing telephone, or the fire alarm by different patterns of vibration. This system can also be linked to fans or a flashing of the room lights to provide other clues.

Building management

Maintenance and renovation

After a period of a few years, any building will require redecoration, refurnishing, perhaps some additional fittings, maybe even complete renovation. The building designers originally involved will have moved on and those now responsible may not be aware of the thinking behind many of the original installations and provisions.

The temptation to create a fresh look runs the risk of undoing a lot of good work: for example, the re-carpeting of a staircase might involve forgetting the nosing.

It is important, therefore, that there should be permanent records of the specification of the internal finishing of the building, together with some explanatory notes.

Commercial buildings should set up regular inspection routines to ensure that all aspects of a building are kept to a good standard of repair. This approach can help prevent accidents and major repair bills whilst enabling expenditure to be planned and controlled as part of the overall management accounts.

Where sometimes hard-won improvements for disabled people have been incorporated, it is essential that standards are maintained and not allowed progressively to decline through indifference or insensitivity.

Organisational culture

Inevitably the question of organisational culture arises. Encouraging proper attitudes is as important as installing appropriate equipment. Often building managers cannot rely solely on the provision of good facilities and effective maintenance. It may be necessary to train staff to observe people using the building, to notice whether they have disabilities and identify any additional assistance that might be needed.

Consider the actual example of a prestigious hotel which has excellent fire precautions and emergency procedures. Behind its reception desk a sign with large lettering says, 'If you are likely to require assistance in the event of an emergency, please advise the receptionist when you check in'. This is of no use to a visually impaired person and unless staff are trained to identify the symptoms of visual impairment and give a verbal explanation, their most susceptible guests are disadvantaged.

Similarly, a receptionist giving directional instructions should be made aware that using phrases such as 'over there', 'in that direction', or simply pointing, is of little help to a visually impaired person.

Good housekeeping

Housekeeping affects the appearance, efficiency and safety of any building. Systems and procedures should be established from the outset to ensure good practice. Here are a few suggestions:

- boxes of stationery in stores should not be left in entrances and corridors;

- fire escapes must never be blocked;

- doors must not be propped open with waste bins;

- fire extinguishers should be checked on a regular planned basis;

- filing cabinet drawers must not be routinely left open;

- dirty or unrepaired light fittings and windows will cancel the designer's best lighting decisions.

It is not within the scope of this book to recommend how good building maintenance and housekeeping might be achieved. However we raise these issues simply because it is important to stress that good building design does not stop with prescription - to be successful it must be sustained in use.

Appendices

a: **How the eye works**

To understand the complexities of visual loss, it is essential
to acquire a basic knowledge of how the human visual
system works and how scenes are viewed and interpreted
by the eye and the brain.

The illustration on the next page represents a simplified
cross-section of the eye and how the passage of light is
altered as it penetrates the eyeball. In a normal eye the rays
of light will be brought to a fine focus to produce a sharp
image on the retina. Here it is converted into electrical
energy and transmitted to the brain via the optic pathways.

It is interesting to note that what is seen on the left of centre
in both eyes is interpreted by the right half of the brain and
vice versa. In other words the world perceived by the eye is
divided vertically and sent to opposite sides of the brain
(ie both left halves to the right visual cortex and both right
halves to the left visual cortex). This is demonstrated in the
diagram on the next page.

The workings of the human eye are analogous to that of a
camera. Light entering the eye must pass through the clear
window at the front which is known as the cornea. As it
does so, the initial bending of light rays takes place as a first
stage towards the production of a clear image on the
membrane at the back of the eye which is known as the
retina. This is a thin membrane which lines the inner wall
of the eyeball, and equates to a 'film' in a camera, upon

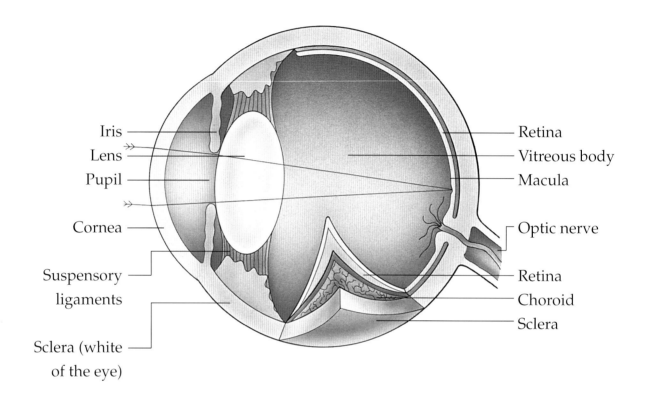

Cross section of the eye

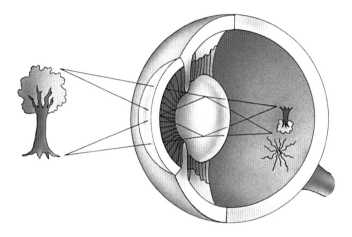

The eye works in similiar fashion to a camera, working to produce a sharp image on the retina. An image focused on the macula area of the retina enables us to see fine detail.

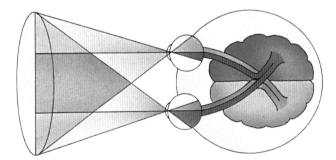

The world perceived by the eye is divided vertically, and information from the left half of vision in each eye is sent to the right visual cortex, and both right halves of vision to the left visual cortex.

which a sharp image must be produced. The 'fine tuning' of these light rays is undertaken by the lens, which just like the lens in a camera, focuses the image on the film plane (retina). It is essential that just the right amount of light enters the eye, so the number of rays is controlled by the iris, a curtain-like material that operates in a similar fashion to the aperture in a camera.

On a dull day the aperture is opened up to allow more light to reach the film and on a bright day it is closed down to restrict the amount of light reaching the film. The iris in the eye operates in the same way, opening and closing the pupil to ensure that just the correct amount of light reaches the retina.

Once a sharp image has been produced on the retina it must be transmitted to the visual cortex area of the brain to be interpreted. The cells in the retina work in a very similar way to those in a light meter. Light falling onto the cells is converted into electrical impulses which are fed along very fine hair-like nerves. These nerves are brought together at the back of the eye to form the optic nerve which then transmits this electrical energy to the brain for interpretation.

This explanation has of necessity been very much simplified but nevertheless it conveys the basic idea of how the human visual system operates.

'What' and 'where' vision
As indicated, above the retina is a thin membrane which lines the inner wall of the eyeball. It consists of millions of light sensitive cells which consist of two types: rods and cones. Cone cells have their greatest concentration around

the central area of the retina and become less and less common the closer to the periphery of our field of view they are situated. Generally speaking, cone cells are highly sensitive to colour but not so sensitive to light. They give us our ability to see fine detail and to differentiate between subtle variations in colour. The densest concentration of cone cells occurs right in the centre of our visual field and is known as the macula.

Rod cells on the other hand have their greatest concentration around the peripheral area of the retina. Rod cells are not very sensitive to colour but are highly sensitive to light and give us our ability to see where things are in relation to ourselves and to each other and enable us to see in the dark.

It will be apparent that peripheral vision enables us to locate ourselves within our environment. It gives us our ability to see where objects are in relation to us and in relation to each other and generally guides our movements through a given area or task. In short this area of vision can be referred to as our 'where' vision. Central vision on the other hand gives us our ability to see fine detail and generally defines exactly what we are looking at. It can therefore be defined as our 'what' vision. As we walk down the street and something catches the corner of our eye, we know where it is but it is necessary to turn our head or eye to look directly at the object in order to determine what it is.

158

b: Useful Information

Lighting Code Of Practice
1994 CIBSE Code for Interior Lighting is published by the Chartered Institution of Building Services Engineers, 222 Balham High Road, London SW12 9BS. Telephone 0181 675 5211.

React System/Tactile Maps
Maps & Diagram Department, RNIB Production & Distribution Centre, Bakewell Road, Orton Southgate, Peterborough PE2 6XU. Telephone 01733 370777. Charges and 'turnaround' times vary according to needs - just send 'basic plan'.

Tactile Audio Braille Services, YPI Building, 83-93 George Street, Hull HU1 3BM. Telephone 01482 585383.

Braille and Embossed Signs and Notices
Brand ID, 357 Bolton Road, Edgworth, Turton, Lancs. BL7 0AZ. Telephone 01204 853003.

Graphex Industrial Art Limited, Roslin Road, South Acton Industrial Estate, London W3 8BW. Telephone 0181 992 7083.

Hagger Electronics, Unit 22, Business Centre West, Avenue 1, Letchworth, Herts. SG6 2HB. Telephone 01462 677331.

Modulex Systems Limited, North Portway Close, Round Spinney, Northampton NN3 4RR. Product Manager: Telephone 01604 494222.

Service Call, Millford Lane, Bakewell, Derbyshire DE4 1DX.
Telephone 01629 812422.

Seton Limited, Department Z, PO Box 77, Banbury, Oxon
OX16 7LS. Telephone 01295 269955.

The Sign Design Society, 66 Derwent Road, Kingsbourne Green,
Harpenden, Herts. AL5 3NX. Telephone & Fax 01582 713556.

Tactyle, Mallard House, The Old Station, Little Bealings,
Woodbridge, Suffolk IP13 6CT. Telephone 01473 620100.

Talking Signs, Unit 6, Littleroyd Mills, Queens Mill Road,
Huddersfield HD1 3DG. Telephone 01484 427232.

A Code of Practice governing the design and specification of
tactile and braille signs should be published shortly.
For information, contact The Sign Design Society, or RNIB,
telephone 0171 388 1266.

Talking Noticeboards
'Self Talker' European Solutions, PO Box 10, Mortimer,
Reading, Berkshire RG7 2QL. Telephone 01734 883607,
fax 01734 885468.

Task Lighting details
The Partially Sighted Society, 62 Salusbury Road, London
NW6 6NS. Telephone 0171 372 1551.
Mail order Partially Sighted Society, Queen's Road,
Doncaster DN1 2NX. Telephone 01302 323132/368998.
Payment with order, price includes post and packing for UK
Mainland only. For copy of free brochure and catalogue,
send a 12" x 9" s.a.e. to the Doncaster office.

Cooker Panels and Controls for Brailling

Customers are advised to have the supplier send the necessary components to RNIB Production & Distribution Centre, Bakewell Road, Orton Southgate, Peterborough PE2 6XU, telephone 01733 370777, where they are studded or brailled as required.

Furniture

Bedroom furniture, suitable for visually impaired persons, can be obtained from John Pulsford Associates Limited, Contracts International House, 28-32 Britannia Street, London WC1X 9JF. Telephone 0171 837 3399, fax 0171 278 0802.

Aids for deafblind people

The 'TAM', a lightweight sound monitor for profoundly deaf people. Details can be obtained from the manufacturer, Summit, 74 Wheeleys Road, Edgbaston, Birmingham B15 2LN. Telephone 0121 440 8078.

(The device is free of VAT to people with hearing loss.)

'Brailtalk' enables sighted children and adults to understand braille and recently blinded people to come to terms with braille. It can also help anyone to communicate with a person who is both deaf and blind.

Contact Electronic Services for the Blind, 28 Crofton Avenue, Orpington, Kent BR6 8DU. Telephone (day) 01732 64128, (evenings/weekends) 01689 855651.

Leaflets on installing 'Induction loops in public places', 'Radios and Infra-Red Hearing Aid Systems', and 'Help with TV' are available from RNID, 105 Gower Street, London WC1E 6AH. Telephone 0171 387 8033, or 9 Clairmont Gardens, Glasgow G3 7LW. Telephone 0141 332 0343.

Vibrating fire alarm available from Priory Fire Protection. Telephone 013225 57727.

General
For advice on disabled facility grants for adaptations to housing, contact RNIB Housing Service, Garrow House, 190 Kensal Road, London W10 5BT. Telephone 0181 969 2380.

For advice on obtaining access audits, etc., contact RNIB/GDBA Joint Mobility Unit, 224 Great Portland Street, London W1N 6AA. Telephone 0171 388 1266.

The Centre for Accessible Environments (formerly Centre on Environment for the Handicapped) address is Nutmeg House, 60 Gainsford Street, London SE1 2NY. Telephone 0171 357 8182. Provides information on the design of environments which are accessible to all.

Information on local and national organisations of blind, partially sighted and deafblind people can be obtained from RNIB, 224 Great Portland Street, London W1N 6AA. Telephone 0171 388 1266.

162

c: Bibliography

ACCESS COMMITTEE FOR ENGLAND. Working together for access: a manual for access groups. London: ACE, 1992. 2pp.

ACCESS COMMITTEE FOR ENGLAND. Building homes for successive generations. London: ACE, 1992.

ADAMS, G.R. The blind and partially sighted. In K. Bayes and S. Francklin, editors. Designing for the handicapped, 47-50. London: George Godwin, 1971.

ADAMS, G.R. The design of buildings for the blind. Unpublished thesis, 1967. 196pp.

AIELLO, J. and STEINFELD, E. Accessible buildings for people with severe visual impairments; prepared for US Department of Housing and Urban Development under Contract H-2200 to Syracuse University. Washington, DC: US Government Printing Office, April 1979. iv, 118pp.

ALLEN, Jill. The blind in the traffic environment. Arrive, September 1978, 2(18), 14-15.

ALLEN, Jill. Environment. Viewpoint, October/December 1981, 55-58.

AMERICAN ASSOCIATION OF WORKERS FOR THE BLIND. Architectural hazards encountered by visually handicapped travellers. Mahwah, N.J.: AAWB Interest Group No. 9, New York State Chapter, n.d. (c.1977). 14pp

AMERICAN ASSOCIATION OF WORKERS FOR THE BLIND. Interest Group 9. Committee on Architectural and Environmental Concerns of the Visually Impaired. Guidelines: architectural and environmental concerns of the visually impaired person. Fullerton, CA: AAWB, 1977. viii, 44pp.

AMERICAN FOUNDATION FOR THE BLIND. Accommodation and accessibility: implementing the ADA on a local level. Journal of Visual Impairment and Blindness, September 1992, 86(7), supplement. 20pp.

BANERJI, M. Buildings for the blind. Blind Welfare (Bombay), April 1982, 24(1), 2-7.

BARRICK, J., COOPER, S., CROWTHER, N., SHARPE, K.
The housing needs of people with a visual impairment, London:
The Housing Corporation, 1995. 65pp.

BARRICK, J. The refurbishment of the Sir Nicholas Garrow House
Hostel for the Blind and Visually Handicapped. News and Views of
Hostels, 1990, No. 2 April/May, pp13-16.

BAYES, K. and FRANCKLIN, S., editors. Designing for the
handicapped. London: George Godwin, 1971. 79pp.

BENTZEN, Billie Louise. Accessibility guidelines for blindness
professionals. Yearbook of the AERBVI, 1984, 2, 2-12.

BENTZEN, Billie Louise and others. Solutions for problems of
visually impaired users of rail rapid transit: Volume I of II concerning
improving communications with the visually impaired in rail rapid
transit systems; prepared for US Department of Transportation, Urban
Mass Transportation Administration, Office of Policy Research.
Washington, DC: US DOT/UMTA, August 1981. v.p. (273pp.)

Information about visual impairment for architects and transit
planners: Volume II of II concerning improving communications, etc.
ii, 57pp.

BERNARDO, J.R. Architecture for blind persons. New Outlook for
the Blind, October 1970, 64(8), 262-265.

Blind misleading the blind. Braille Forum, August 1984, 23(2), 19-20.

BLIND MOBILITY RESEARCH UNIT. Report to the Department of
Transport on the enhancement of the visibility of street furniture.
(BMRU Report No. 74) Nottingham: BMRU, Department of
Psychology, University of Nottingham, September 1981. 5pp.

BOBROVA, Tatiana. Architecture for visually handicapped persons.
Review of the European Blind, 1990, 19(4), 70th issue, 24-33. Fr, Eng,
Rus, Ger.

BOYCE, P.R. Lighting for the partially sighted: some observations in a
residential home. (Capenhurst research memorandum ECRC/M1980).
Chester: Electricity Council, January 1986. 40pp.

BRABYN, J.A. and BRABYN, Lesley A. Speech intelligibility of the
talking signs. Journal of Visual Impairment and Blindness, February
1982, 76(2), 77-78.

164

BRABYN, Lesley A. and BRABYN, J.A. An evaluation of 'Talking Signs' for the blind. Human Factors, 1983, 25(1), 49-53.

BRAF, P. The physical environment and the visually impaired: the planning and adaptation of buildings and other forms of physical environment for visually impaired people. Bromma, Sweden: ICTA Information Centre, 1974. 34pp.

BRISTOW, A., RUTHERFORD, A. A survey of housing designed for people who have a physical disability. London: DOE, 1979.

BRITISH BROADCASTING CORPORATION. BBC 'In Touch' catalogue [for] a kitchen for the visually handicapped at the Disabled Living Foundation ... London: BBC/DLF, February 1985. 26pp. appendix.

BRITISH RAILWAYS BOARD. Department of Architecture and Design. Station design guide for disabled customers. Croydon: British Railways Board, 1989, 14pp.

BRITISH STANDARDS INSTITUTION. Code of practice for access for the disabled to buildings (formerly CP96: Part 1). BS 5810:1979. London: BSI, 1979. i, 14pp.

BRITISH STANDARDS INSTITUTION. Code of practice for design of housing for the convenience of disabled people. BS 5619:1978. London: BSI, 1978. 6pp.

BRITISH STANDARDS INSTITUTION. Draft BS for fire precautions in the design and construction of buildings. Part 8: code of practice for means of escape for disabled people. London: BSI, December 1985. ii, 30pp.

BRODEY, W. Sound and space. New Outlook for the Blind, January 1965, 59(1), 1-4.

Building for the disabled. Contact (CCD), November/December 1976, 3(8), 6-8.

BRUCE, I., McKENNELL, A. and WALKER, E. Blind and partially sighted adults in Britain: the RNIB survey Vol.1, HMSO, London 1991.

CARDWELL, H. Barriers to mobility. Journal of Visual Impairment and Blindness, December 1977, 71(10) 463-464.

CATT, R. Planning the home environment for the partially sighted: Parts 1 and 2. Foresight No. 2, 5 December 1980, 4-5; No. 3, 21 January 1981, 4,10. Reprinted in Oculus, September/October 1981, 98; November/December 1981, 105-108.

CENTRE ON ENVIRONMENT FOR THE HANDICAPPED. Designing buildings to accommodate the needs of people with disabilities: an updated summary of the legislation and official guidance. London: CEH, October 1989. Unpaged (2pp.) Typescript.

CENTRE ON ENVIRONMENT FOR THE HANDICAPPED. Designing for people with sensory handicaps: bibliography 5. London: CEH, February 1981. 24pp.

CHEN, Jen-Gwo and HOU, Chien-An. A computerised system for workplace design for visually impaired workers: short report. Journal of Visual Impairment and Blindness, May 1991, 85(5), 232-233.

CHOMARAT, D. Architecture et handicapes: le cas de l'aveugle. Comme les Autres No. 72, 2e trimestre 1982, 11-13.

COHN, H.H. Greater protection for the disabled against public street works hazards. Viewpoint, 1985, Winter issue, 51, 53, 55.

COLQUHOUN, I. and SHEPHERD, J. Housing for disabled people. 1988. London. IOH,RIBA.

COOPER, Barbara Acheson. A model for implementing color contrast in the environment of the elderly. American Journal of Occupational Therapy, 39(4), 253-258.

COUNCIL OF EUROPE. Resolution and report on the adaptation of housing and surrounding areas to the needs of disabled persons. Strasbourg: Council of Europe, January 1979. 46pp.

CRAIN-REVIS ASSOCIATES, INC. and the WASHINGTON CONSULTING GROUP. A handbook describing low cost concepts and techniques to make public transportation more accessible for visually and hearing impaired persons; prepared under contract for US Department of Transportation, Urban Mass Transportation Administration, Office of Service and Management Demonstrations. Washington, DC: US DOT/UMTA, April 1982. iv, 54pp.

CWMBRAN DEVELOPMENT CORPORATION. A guide to housing services for the disabled, 2nd edition. Cwmbran: Torfaen Borough Council and Cwmbran Development Corporation, 1984 (first published 1979). 12pp.

166

DeCARO, J.J. Design of access: implications for disabled people, GLAD News, July 1980, 5(3), 3-5.

DEPARTMENT OF THE ENVIRONMENT. House adaptations for people with physical disabilities. London: HMSO 1988.

Design of kitchens for blind persons. New Outlook for the Blind, December 1976, 70(10), 428.

DIALOGUE WITH THE BLIND. A handbook on tactile signs and location cues for the blind and visually impaired. Berwyn, IL: Dialogue with the Blind, 1978. 16pp.

DICKMAN, I.R. Making life more livable: simple adaptations for the homes of blind and visually impaired older people. New York: American Foundation for the Blind, 1983. 92pp. Large print.

DISABLEMENT INCOME GROUP CHARITABLE TRUST. Tell me what you want and I'll get it for you: a study of shopping when disabled. London: DIG Charitable Trust, 1983. 15pp.

DUNCAN, J, and others. Environmental modifications for the visually impaired: a handbook. Journal of Visual Impairment and Blindness, December 1977, 71(10), 441-455.

ENGLISH TOURIST BOARD. Providing for visitors with impaired vision: advice to hotel and guesthouse proprietors on meeting the needs of visitors with impaired vision. London: ETB, 1981. Folder.

The environment of blind people: report of CEH* seminar held on 29 April 1975. CEH Newsletter 7, May 1975, 32-36. *Centre on Environment for the Handicapped.

FERGUSON, Roy V. Environmental design for disabled persons.   In Roy I. Brown, editor. Quality of life for handicapped people, 164-183. London: Croom Helm, 1988.

FETHERSTONE, J.M. Building for the blind. Unpublished thesis, n.d.(c.1958). 52pp.

FILLER, M. Extra sensory perceptions: house near New York. Progressive Architecture, April 1978, 59(4), 82-85.

FILPUS, P. Unique mobility hazards. Braille Forum, March 1981, 19(9), 12-14.

FINCH, Jessica. Contrasts. New Beacon, September 1980, 64(761), 225-227.

FLANDER, M.J. Pathfinder tiles. Braille Forum, April 1986, 24(10), 16-20.

FORD, Margaret. In touch at home. Oxford: Isis Large Print, 1986. xii, 87pp.

FORDREE, J. The Papworth story: rehabilitation with employment opportunities. Rehab Network No. 4, Winter 1986, 3-4.

FRYE, Ann. Developments in tactile surfaces for pedestrians. British Journal of Visual Impairment, Spring 1990, 8(1), 36-37.

GALKOWSKI, A. Architects supporting integration of the disabled within the community. International Journal of Rehabilitation Research, 1987, 10(4), supplement 5. Proceedings of the second European conference on research in rehabilitation, Düsseldorf 18-19 November 1985, 220-224.

GALLON, Christine and others. Tactile footway surfaces for the blind; by Christine Gallon, Philip Oxley and Barbara Simms. Viewpoint, October 1991, 45(201), 33-35.

GAZELY, D. The use of contrast as an aid to low vision. Oculus, July/August 1983, 7(4), 62-27.

A geriatric home for the blind: voluntary enterprise in a successful experiment: [Pocklington House, Northwood, Middlesex]. British Hospital and Social Service Journal, 25 October 1963, 1300-1302.

GILL, John Martin. New technology for general use: some implications for visually disabled persons. Technical Development Newsletter No 4, May 1990, 8-10.

GOLDSMITH, S. Designing for the disabled, 2nd ed. New York: McGraw-Hill, 1967.

GREAT BRITAIN. Acts. Disabled Persons Act 1981. Chapter 43. London: HMSO, 1981. i, 9pp.

GREAT BRITAIN. Statutory Instruments. Building and Buildings: the Building (Disabled People) Regulations 1987. S.I. 1987 No. 1445. London: HMSO, 1987. 3pp.

GREAT BRITAIN. Department of Health. Social Services Inspectorate. Caring for quality: guidance on standards for residential homes for people with physical disability. London: HMSO, 1990. 38pp.

168

GREATER LONDON ASSOCIATION FOR DISABLED PEOPLE.
Access: regulations and guidelines. Guides to information, Number 3,
1987. London: GLAD, 1987. 4pp.

GREATER LONDON ASSOCIATION FOR THE DISABLED. Into the
eighties: access to the built environment: symposium papers given at
The Polytechnic of the South Bank, Thursday, June 5th 1980. London:
GLAD, 1981. 24pp.

GREENHALGH, R. Help yourself to see. Oculus, July/August 1982,
6(4), 62-63.

HAMPSON, R. and others. Caught in the turbulence: care in the
community. Community Care, 9 May 1985, 20-22.

HARRISON, Lyn and MEANS, Robin. Housing: the essential
element in community care. Oxford: Anchor Trust, 1990. xii, 96pp.

HELLMAN, Louis. There's none so blind: [Royal Leicestershire,
Rutland and Wycliffe Society for the Blind Resources Centre]
Architects' Journal, 2 March 1988, 42-45, 47.

HERTFORDSHIRE SOCIETY FOR THE BLIND. Access for people
with impaired vision: notes on design features which can be helpful
and on those which can limit independence. Hertford: The Society,
1984. 4pp. Typescript.

HIGGERTY, Moira. The physical environment and the visually
impaired. Imfama, June 1983, 23(3), 1-3.

HOLLADAY, David. Braille on signs. Raised Dot Computing
Newsletter, January- February 1992, 10(94), 3-4.

Hostel for the blind: winning entry in Norwich competition. Building,
29 November 1966, 67-69.

HOWELL, M. Below the belt. New Beacon, March 1985, 69(815), 77-80.

HUGHES, S. Disabled travellers: British Rail's approach. Viewpoint,
Summer 1986, 81, 83, 85, 87.

**ICTA INFORMATION CENTRE and ROYAL ASSOCIATION FOR
DISABILITY AND REHABILITATION.** Guidelines for improving
access for disabled people (Directives pour une meilleure accessibilité
de l'environnement aux personnes handicapées). Bromma, Sweden: ICTA
Information Centre/London: RADAR, 1983. Folder.

INSTITUTION OF HIGHWAYS AND TRANSPORTATION.
Guidelines for providing for people with a mobility handicap. London:
The Institution, February 1986. 48pp.

INTERNATIONAL ORGANIZATION FOR STANDARDIZATION.
Needs of disabled people in buildings: design guidelines. Geneva: ISO,
1982. 19pp.

JACKSON, R.M. and others. Visually handicapped travellers in the
rapid rail transit environment. Journal of Visual Impairment and
Blindness, December 1983, 77(10), 469-475.

JAGER, Johann. Participation in planning and administration: the first
cultural and recreational centre for the blind in Austria. Review of the
European Blind, 1988, 17(4), 62nd issue, 16-25. Fr, Eng, Rus, Ger.

JAMES, G.A. A map of the Victoria Centre, Nottingham: teaching
guidelines. Nottingham: Blind Mobility Research Unit, Department of
Psychology, University of Nottingham, n.d. (1975). 4pp.

JAMES, G.A. and WILLSON, G.T. Visual impairment and the
physical environment: resource organisations, legislation and an
annotated bibliography. London: Joint Committee on Mobility of Blind
and Partially Sighted People, January 1980. 10pp. Computer printout.
(Revised August 1980, 12pp.)

JENSEN, Svend. Danish architecture for the blind. Review of the
European Blind, 1990, 19(1), 67th issue, 22-25. Fr, Eng, Rus, Ger.

JOFFEE, Elga. Visually impaired travellers: the suburban
environment: comment. Journal of Visual Impairment and Blindness,
December 1984, 78(10), 493.

KLEMZ, Astrid. Glowing in the dark: home news. New Beacon, May
1985, 69(817), 147-148.

KLEMZ, Astrid. Hazards to the blind and partially sighted: 1.
Roadworks and obstructions on the footway. 2. How blind people
travel. London: London Borough of Waltham Forest, January 1977.
4pp. Typescript.

LaGROW, S.J. and BARTON, L.E. Visibility factors affecting
discrimination by visually impaired persons. The Mental Retardation
and Learning Disability Bulletin, 1984, 12, 87-97.

LAPPIN, Nicky. Rotherhithe Youth Hostel: building study. Access by
Design No 58, May/August 1992, 6-9.

LARGE, P. Providing supportive services: the physical environment - housing, outdoor mobility and access: Unit 13. In Open University. Providing supportive services: Units 12-13 [of] 'The handicapped person in the community'. 57- 99. Milton Keynes: Open University Press, 1975.

LEONARD, E. The handicapped building. Rehabilitation Literature, September 1978, 39(9), 265-269.

LIBRARY OF CONGRESS. National Library Service for the Blind and Physically Handicapped. Planning barrier free libraries: a guide for renovation and construction of libraries serving blind and physically handicapped readers. Washington, DC: LC/NLS, 1981. iv, 61pp. Large print.

LIDDICOAT, Catherine M. and others. A comparison of two sets of non-braille elevator symbols. Journal of Visual Impairment and Blindness, May 1982, 76(5), 194-196.

LINDSTROM, J. Hints to planners of the environment for the visually handicapped. Review of the European Blind 1978, 7(2), 20th issue, 10-16.

LINDSTROM, J. and LINDQVIST, B. Physical planning for the visually impaired. In Report on Conference on Technical Aids for the Blind, London, April 1977. 12pp.

LONDON: HARINGEY. 'Not everyone can see', April 1979 to October 1979: Haringey Council's campaign for the visually handicapped. London: London Borough of Haringey Public Relations Office, 1980.

LONDON: HARROW. Department of Development and Technical Services. Planning for the disabled. London: London Borough of Harrow, n.d. (1978). 21pp.

LONDON: ISLINGTON. Housing for people with disabilities, a design guide. LBI Architectural department, 1989.

LONDON STRATEGIC POLICY UNIT. Planning policy group toward integration: the participation of people with disabilities in planning. London: The Unit/London Borough Disability Resource Team, 1988. 96pp.

LORD, K. Kerb ramping. Imfama, June 1984, 24(3), 9-10.

LORENTE, J. The planning of buildings and towns for the blind and visually handicapped. In Report on Conference on Technical Aids for the Blind, London, April 1977. 5pp.

LOUGHBOROUGH, W. Talking lights. Journal of Visual Impairment and Blindness, June 1979, 73(6), 243.

LOZANO, E. and IBARBIA, E. Greater pedestrian safety through use of Pathfinder Tiles. Braille Forum, June 1985, 23(12), 22-24.

MASON, Wendy and HOGBEN, Mary. The Crowndale Centre, London: building study. Access by Design No. 52, May/August 1990, 6-11.

McELROY, J.F. Building for the blind: the architecture, heating and ventilation, best adapted to their needs. In Proceedings of the 9th Biennial Meeting of the American Association of Instructors of the Blind, New York, 1986, 11-25.

McGILLIVRAY, R. Making the environment more visible for the elderly visually impaired. Aids and Appliances Review No. 13, Summer 1984, 5-10.

McGLINCHEY, M.A. and MITALA, R.F. Using environmental design to teach ward layout to severely and profoundly retarded blind persons: a proposal. New Outlook for the Blind, April 1975, 69(4), 168-171.

METTLER, Richard. Blindness and managing the environment. Journal of Visual Impairment and Blindness, December 1987, 81(10), 476-481.

MIDDLESBROUGH BOROUGH COUNCIL. Access for all: progress report 1982-1985. Middlesbrough: Middlesbrough BC, 1985. 13pp.

MILLER, G. Subway safety in New York City. Journal of Visual Impairment and Blindness, December 1983, 77(10), 474-475.

MILNER, Margaret. Toward an accessible environment: a review of recent developments. Blindness (AAWB Annual), 1977-78, 8-14.

Modifying the environment at home. Journal of Visual Impairment and Blindness, March 1977, 71(3), 121.

MONTAN, K. A better urban environment for people with visual impairment. Rehabilitation Literature, January 1969, 30(1), 14-15.

172

MURRAY, H. Atlanta Airport designed with handicapped users in mind. Braille Forum, June 1982, 20(12), 9-13. Large print.

'Musical pathway' helps visually impaired elderly persons maintain independence. Mainstream, Summer 1987, 14(3), 2-3.

NATIONAL ARTS & HANDICAPPED INFORMATION SERVICE. Architectural accessibility. Materials from the National Arts & the Handicapped Information Service, October 1977, 1-23.

NATIONAL CONSUMER COUNCIL. Getting around: the barriers to access for disabled people. London: The Council, 1981. vi, 42pp.

NEE, Pauline. Access in the USA: designing for people with disabilities. London: Royal Institution of Chartered Surveyors, 1990. 33pp.

Needing a push: how the arts neglect the disabled: a report based on a study of the Greenwich Festival. London: Greater London Arts Association in collaboration with the Greater London Association for the Disabled, 1979. 27pp.

NELSON, Barbara. Californians battle for subway safety. Braille Forum, October 1984, 23(4), 17-19.

Norwich Home for the Blind: competition award. Architect and Building News, 30 November 1966, 947-950.

NULL, Roberta. Environmental design for the low-vision elderly. Journal of Home Economics, Fall 1988, 80(3), 29-35.

NULL, Roberta. Model kitchen design for the low vision elderly community. Journal of Visual Impairment and Blindness, June 1988, 82(6), 240-245.

Notes of a seminar held on 11 October 1982 by the National Federation of the Blind and the Department of Transport as part of the NFB's Pavement Week. Viewpoint, October/November 1983, Autumn issue, 59, 61, 63, 65.

ONTARIO DEPARTMENT OF EDUCATION. School Planning and Building Research Section. Soundstop: an experimental student housing study [for deaf and blind students]. Toronto: The Department, 1969. 40pp.

PALFREYMAN, Tessa. A day at the Dome [Doncaster Leisure Centre]. Access by Design No. 52, May/August 1990, 18-21.

PARTIALLY SIGHTED SOCIETY. Providing for people with impaired vision: access guide: advice to stores, banks, offices and transport systems on meeting the needs of visually disabled people. Doncaster: PSS, 1985. 12pp.

PARTIALLY SIGHTED SOCIETY. Providing for people with impaired vision. Doncaster: the Society, 1991. 8pp.

PASSINI, Romedi and PROULX, Guylene. Building access and safety for the visually impaired person. In J.D. Sime, editor. Safety in the built environment, 116-129. London: E.&F.N. Spon, 1988. Typescript.

PASSINI, Romedi and others. The spatio-cognitive abilities of the visually impaired population. Environment and Behaviour, January 1990, 22(1), 91-118.

PASSINI, Romedi. Wayfinding information for congenitally blind individuals: short report. Journal of Visual Impairment and Blindness, December 1988, 82(10), 425-429.

PASSINI, R. and others. Spatial mobility of the visually handicapped active person: a descriptive study: short report. Journal of Visual Impairment and Blindness, October 1986, 80(8), 904-907.

PASTALAN, L.A. The simulation of age-related sensory losses: a new approach to the study of environmental barriers. New Outlook for the Blind, October 1974, 68(8), 356-362.

PATTERSON, E.W. Give us back our pavements. Viewpoint, January/March 1979, Winter issue, 31-33.

Pavement Day seminar held on 6 June 1984 at the Department of Transport. Viewpoint, 1985, Winter issue, 33, 35, 37, 39-41, 43,45.

PEARSON, Anne. Arts for everyone: guidance on provision for disabled people. Dunfermline: Carnegie UK Trust/London: Centre on Environment for the Handicapped, [1985]. vi, 110pp.

PENTON, John H. Providing accessible accommodation: tourism for all; illustrations by M Burrows. London: English Tourist Board; Horley, Surrey: Holiday Care Service, 1990. 48pp.

174

PENTON, John H. RNIB Vocational College, Loughborough: building study. Access by Design no 54, January/April 1991, 5-8.

PORTER, M. and ROBINSON, D. Tyne and Wear Metro, Haymarket-Tynemouth via Benton: Metro access guide for disabled people: a guide to assist wheelchair users, people with sight difficulties and parents with prams or pushchairs. Newcastle upon Tyne: Handicapped Persons Research Unit, Newcastle upon Tyne Polytechnic, March 1981. i, 37pp.

PREISER, W.F.E. and others. A combined tactile/electronic guidance system for the visually handicapped. In Proceedings of the first international symposium on maps and graphics for the visually handicapped ... 1983, Washington, DC, 86-89. Washington, DC: Association of American Geographers, 1983.

PRESCOTT-CLARKE, Patricia. Organising house adaptations for disabled people: a research study [commissioned jointly by the Department of the Environment, Department of Health and Social Security and Welsh Office and undertaken for them by Social and Community Planning Research]. London: HMSO, 1982. iv, 46pp. 2 questionnaires (12pp. and 11pp.)

PRINCE OF WALES' ADVISORY GROUP ON DISABILITY. Living options: guidelines for those planning services for people with severe physical disabilities. London: Prince of Wales' Advisory Group on Disability, 1985. Unpaged. (12pp.).

PROUD, Geoffrey. Pattern for navigation. Health Service Journal, 8 June 1989, 696-697.

PUSWA* Review: oral evidence for associations representing the blind and disabled ... 24 October 1984. Viewpoint, 1985, Spring issue, 61, 63, 65, 67. (*Public Utilities Street Works Act)

QUIN, P. Pocklington. New Beacon, December 1985, 69(824), 365-366. Residential accommodation for the blind: home for blind persons, Pocklington Place, Birmingham. Architects' Journal, 12 September 1973, 599-614.

RIPLEY, W.J. Environmental communication and orientation: twin barriers for the visually, mentally and aurally impaired. North Carolina Architect, September/October 1977, 8-12.

ROBERTSON, N. The great Brent obstacle race. Inter-Regional Review No. 68, Winter 1980/81, 14-16.

ROBINS, Pat. Think before you move. New Beacon, December 1991, 75(893), 475-476.

ROBSON, H. The urban environment. New Beacon, August 1978, 62(736), 197-199.

ROYAL INSTITUTE OF BRITISH ARCHITECTS. Visual handicap: a broadsheet from the Eastern Region Royal Institute of British Architects: sponsored by the Hertfordshire Society for the Blind; written and designed by John Penton. London: RIBA Clients Advisory Service, 1984. Broadsheet.

ROYAL NATIONAL INSTITUTE FOR THE BLIND. Designing buildings for blind people. London: RNIB, November 1985. 8pp.

SAKAMOTO, Lori and MEHR, E.B. A new method of stair markings for visually impaired people: short report. Journal of Visual Impairment and Blindness, January 1988, 82(1), 24-27.

SALMON, F.C. and SALMON, C.F. The blind: space needs for rehabilitation. Stillwater: Oklahoma State University, 1964. 82pp.

SAUNDERS, P. Access and adhocery. Design for Special Needs No. 25, May/August 1981, 7-8.

SCARR, Valerie J. Aids to brighten up the shadows. Therapy Weekly, 28 October 1982, 6.

SCARR, Valerie J. Planning guidelines for buildings used by visually handicapped people: LV3. London: Disabled Living Foundation, 1983. i, 4pp.

SENDEN, M. von. Space and sight: the perception of space and shape in the congenitally blind before and after operation; translated by Peter Heath. London: Methuen, 1960. 348pp.

SEVEN, S.M. Environmental interpretation for the visually impaired. Education of the Visually Handicapped, Summer 1980, 12(2), 53-58.

SHIRLEY, I.M. A visit to the 'ideal home'. Inter-Regional Review No. 72, Winter 1982/83, 50-52.

SICURELLA, V.J. Color contrast as an aid for visually handicapped persons. Journal of Visual Impairment and Blindness, June 1977, 71(6), 252-257.

SOKOLOFF, H.D. The planning process and the environment *in* American Foundation for the Blind, Proceedings of the conference on the visually handicapped child who functions on a retarded level, San Francisco, 1971, 26-34.

SOKOLOFF, V.J. Trends affecting designs for service. New Outlook for the Blind, January 1973, 67(1), 21-25.

STANDEN, E.F. Carina. 'Pass, friend.' Viewpoint, January/March 1979, Winter issue, 26-31.

STEWART, Lorelee Sharon. Creating accessibility for the visually impaired: a three part guide for museum staff. Boston, MA: The Author, June 1987. 27pp. Typescript.

TECHNISCHE HOGESCHOOL DELFT and CITY OF BIRMINGHAM POLYTECHNIC. The physical and psychological aspects of tower-block windows: interviewing the blind. In Windows: an interior view, 4.1-4.5. Birmingham: City of Birmingham Polytechnic, 1979.

TEMPLER, J. and ZIMBRING, C. Accessibility for persons with visual impairments: access information bulletin. Washington, DC: National Center for a Barrier Free Environment, 1981. 8pp.

Textured pavements to help blind pedestrians. Viewpoint, October/November 1983, Autumn issue, 29, 31, 33, 35.

THOMSON, N. The adaptation of existing public buildings for use by the handicapped: report on a pilot research project. London: Polytechnic of Central London, Built Environment Research Group, June 1979. 148pp.

THORNTON, W. Tactile textiles. New Beacon, March 1983, 67(791), 67-68.

THORPE, S. Access for disabled people: design guidance notes for developers. London: Centre on Environment for the Handicapped for Access Committee for England, March 1985. 17pp.

THORPE, S. Designing for people with sensory impairments. Centre on Environment for the Handicapped for the Access Committee for England, June 1986. 21pp.

THORPE, S. Access in the High Street: advice on how to make shopping more manageable for disabled people. London: Centre on Environment for the Handicapped, 1981. 16pp.

TICA, Phyllis L. and SHAW, J.A. Barrier-free design: accessibility for the handicapped. (Publication No. 74-3.) New York: Institute for Research and Development in Occupational Education, Center for Advanced Study in Education, The Graduate School and University Center, City University of New York, 1974. iii, 31pp.

U.S. CIVIL SERVICE COMMISSION. Bureau of Recruiting and Examining, Guide for federal agency coordinators in selective placement of the handicapped: identifying and eliminating architectural barriers. (BRE-60) Washington, DC: US/CSC, October 1974. 7pp.

U.S. DEPARTMENT OF TRANSPORT. Federal Aviation Administration. Access travel: airports: a guide to accessibility of terminals. Washington, DC: US Government Printing Office, 1980. 24pp.

UNITED NATIONS. Designing with care: a guide to adaptation of the built environment for disabled persons. New York: UN, January 1983. 103pp.

VANOLI, D.V. Unsighted barriers. Unpublished diploma thesis, 1972. vi, 97pp.

VAUGHN, C EDWIN. The struggle of blind people for self determination. Charles C Thomas, Illinois, USA. 1993.

VAWDA, R.C. Just a set of rooms: a rehabilitation approach to the provision of local authority services for the visually handicapped. British Journal of Visual Impairment, Autumn 1983, 1(2), 2-5.

VLAHAS, Sue. Suggestions in the use of color contrast for low vision persons. Low Vision Abstracts, Spring 1979, 5(1), 7-11.

WARDELL, K.T. Environmental modifications. In R.L. Welsh and B.B. Blasch, editors. Foundations of orientation and mobility, 477-525. New York: American Foundation for the Blind, 1980.

WHITEHOUSE, Anne. Tailor made: [Demand (design and manufacture for disability), workshop set up by London College of Furniture]. Community Care, 19 September 1985, 16-18.

WILSON, C. and others. Home improvement grants: a guide for disabled persons. MS News No. 108, Summer 1981, 12-15.

178

WILSON, Rod. Colour and the visually-impaired rail traveller. New Beacon, February 1989, 73(861), 41-44.

WINNING, Ann S. Give us back our pavements. New Beacon, October 1979, 63(750), 258-259.

ZIMRING, C. and TEMPLER, J. Wayfinding and orientation by the visually impaired. Journal of Environmental Systems, 1983-84, 13(4), 333-352.

RNIB / GBDA Joint Mobility Unit

The Joint Mobility Unit aims to improve building design, pedestrian facilities and transport systems so that blind, partially sighted and deafblind people can move around safely, independently and without undue restriction. Its services are available throughout the UK and include:

- the giving of practical advice, including information packs;

- consultancy services, both for public and private sector organisations seeking to create user accessible environments, including environmental access audits and appraisals;

- education and training, including design courses, supplying speakers and seminar design;

- research and development support to individuals and organisations wishing to establish innovative or mainstream projects and product development in this area.

For further information, please contact:

RNIB/GDBA Joint Mobility Unit,
224 Great Portland Street,
London W1N 6AA

Telephone: 0171 388 1266
Fax: 0171 388 3160

RNIB Housing Service

The RNIB Housing Service's mission is to remove the barriers to housing and to help in providing effective solutions to the housing problems of blind and partially sighted people. The service works with housing providers on a wide range of issues including:

- physical design and access issues

- advice on design manual specifications

- advice on housing management practice

- advice on integrating visually impaired tenants into tenant participation procedures

- training for housing professionals and staff

- advocacy for visually impaired tenants and home owners

For further information, contact:

RNIB Housing Service
Garrow House, 190 Kensal Road, North Kensington,
London W10 5BT.

Tel: 0181 969 2380

Tate House, 28 Wetherby Road, Harrogate,
North Yorkshire HG2 7SA

Telephone: 01423 886927

Peter Barker
BSc, DMS, FBIM

has a degree in Mechanical Engineering and is a Fellow of the British Institute of Management. He worked in Manufacturing for many years and was then a Director of various companies in the building and construction industry.

Being visually impaired, he brought his own personal experience and wider knowledge to RNIB three years ago to set up the RNIB/GDBA Joint Mobility Unit. The Unit provides services covering building design, the pedestrian environment and transport systems with the overall objective of bringing about improvements for visually impaired and deafblind people.

Jon Barrick
BSc, DipHsing, MCIH

has a degree in Social Sciences and is a member of the Chartered Institute of Housing. He has worked in local government in various roles within housing departments, and is currently an Assistant Director with RNIB with responsibility for the Housing and Environmental Services department. He was Head of Service in 1991 when RNIB won the Chartered Institute of Housing's Elis Fisher Award for Housing Management.

With his team, he is currently pioneering innovative collaborative project work between RNIB and the housing movement, encouraging closer links with those who build our environment, and with those who provide care to blind people in managed accommodation.

Rod Wilson
CSS

is a registered blind person. He has worked in the field of visual impairment for nearly thirty years. He was one of the first people in Britain to qualify as an orientation and mobility specialist and worked in the Mobility Department at RNIB's rehabilitation Centre in Torquay, leading on to a responsibility for the development of low vision services.

His last post as Low Vision Development Officer within RNIB involved him in the design and implementation of training courses in low vision and the undertaking of consultancy in all matters concerning the provision of a suitable environment for visually impaired people.